# Treasures of Hope

# Treasures of Hope

By
*Alfred Doerffler*

CONCORDIA PUBLISHING HOUSE

SAINT LOUIS, MISSOURI · 1945

**L**ET the words of my mouth and the meditation of my heart be acceptable in Thy sight, O Lord, my Strength and my Redeemer.

Psalm 19:14.

**T**HOU wilt keep him in perfect peace whose mind is stayed on Thee, because he trusteth in Thee.

Isaiah 26:3.

**L**ET me not be ashamed of my hope.

Psalm 119:116.

**I**N Thy faithfulness answer me.

Psalm 143:1.

# Treasures of Hope

## THE FIRST WEEK

Presented to Mrs John Rempp
Birthday April 1st- 1960
By-
Rev. and Mrs L. G. Mietzner

## Sunday Morning

# Isaiah 55

HO, every one that thirsteth, come ye to the waters! And he that hath no money, come ye, buy, and eat; yea, come, buy wine and milk without money and without price. Wherefore do ye spend money for that which is not bread and your labor for that which satisfieth not? Hearken diligently unto Me, and eat ye that which is good, and let your soul delight itself in fatness.

Incline your ear and come unto Me; hear, and your soul shall live. And I will make an everlasting covenant with you, even the sure mercies of David. Behold, I have given Him for a Witness to the people, a Leader and Commander to the people. Behold, thou shalt call a nation that thou knowest not, and a nation that knew not thee shall run unto thee, because of the Lord, thy God, and for the Holy One of Israel, for He hath glorified thee.

Seek ye the Lord while He may be found; call upon Him while He is near. Let the wicked forsake his way, and the unrighteous man his thoughts; and let him return unto the Lord, and He will have mercy upon him, and to our God, for He will abundantly pardon.

For My thoughts are not your thoughts, neither are your ways My ways, saith the Lord, for as the heavens are higher than the earth, so are My ways higher than your ways and My thoughts than your thoughts. For as the rain cometh down and the snow from heaven and returneth not thither, but watereth the earth and maketh it bring forth and bud, that it may give seed to the sower and bread to the eater, so shall My Word be that goeth forth out of My mouth; it shall not return unto Me void, but shall accomplish that which I please, and it shall prosper in the thing whereto I sent it.

For ye shall go out with joy and be led forth with peace.

# The Morning Prayer

HEAVENLY FATHER, who in Thine abundant goodness and mercy hast given us Thy Word to nourish our immortal souls, grant us the grace to receive Thy message of reconciliation with gladness of heart and to think daily on these saving truths. Thou hast promised that Thy Word shall accomplish its purpose wherever it is proclaimed. Grant that we may grow in grace and knowledge of our Savior, whose love led Him to Calvary to redeem us and make us Thine own.

Turn the hearts of all troubled and distressed souls to Thy ever comforting Gospel, and let all that hear it find peace and forgiveness in Thee.

Bless the preaching of Thy Word in all our churches, and send Thy benediction into our homes, that we may continue to enjoy the Christian graces of contentment, moderation, love, patience, and abide faithfully to the end.

Let Thy Word bear fruit an hundredfold in all our lives. Bless pastors and missionaries, and make our hearts and hands ready and willing to build the kingdom of Thy Son, Jesus Christ, our Lord and Savior, who taught us to pray: Our Father who art in heaven. Amen.

## THE MORNING HYMN

Lord, open Thou my heart to hear
And through Thy Word to me draw near;
Let me Thy Word e'er pure retain,
Let me Thy child and heir remain.

Thy Word doth deeply move my heart,
Thy Word doth perfect health impart,
Thy Word my soul with joy doth bless,
Thy Word brings peace and happiness.

To God the Father, God the Son,
And God the Spirit, Three in One,
Shall glory, praise, and honor be
Now and throughout eternity. Amen.

# Sunday Evening

## Psalm 23

THE Lord is my Shepherd; I shall not want. He maketh me to lie down in green pastures; He leadeth me beside the still waters.

He restoreth my soul.

He leadeth me in the paths of righteousness for His name's sake. Yea, though I walk through the valley of the shadow of death, I will fear no evil, for Thou art with me; Thy rod and Thy staff, they comfort me.

Thou preparest a table before me in the presence of mine enemies. Thou anointest my head with oil; my cup runneth over.

Surely goodness and mercy shall follow me all the days of my life, and I will dwell in the house of the Lord forever.

# The Evening Prayer

AT the close of the day we come to Thee, Shepherd of our souls, to acknowledge Thy loving-kindness and continual guidance. We have been refreshed in the green pastures of Thy Word, strengthened in faith through Thy promises, and healed and restored to Thy grace through the forgiveness of all our sins. With confidence and patience we entrust ourselves to Thy loving care for this night and the coming week, certain that Thy goodness will fill the cup of our daily needs to overflowing and that Thy mercy will guide us into the paths of righteousness, where we can daily live in Thy grace.

Dwell in our midst, and protect us from the many dangers which beset us. Bless us with a refreshing sleep, and fill our souls with peace. Then Thine shall be the praise and the glory, precious Savior, now and to the end of days. Amen.

## THE EVENING HYMN

The King of Love my Shepherd is,
  Whose goodness faileth never;
I nothing lack if I am His,
  And He is mine forever.

Where streams of living water flow,
  My ransomed soul He leadeth,
And where the verdant pastures grow,
  With food celestial feedeth.

Perverse and foolish oft I strayed,
  But yet in love He sought me
And on His shoulder gently laid
  And home, rejoicing, brought me.

In death's dark vale I fear no ill,
  With Thee, dear Lord, beside me;
Thy rod and staff my comfort still,
  Thy cross before to guide me.

Thou spreadst a table in my sight,
  Thy unction grace bestoweth;
And, oh, the transport of delight
  With which my cup o'erfloweth!

And so through all the length of days
  Thy goodness faileth never.
Good Shepherd, may I sing Thy praise
  Within Thy house forever. Amen.

# Monday Morning

## Psalm 1

BLESSED is the man that walketh not in the counsel of the ungodly, nor standeth in the way of sinners, nor sitteth in the seat of the scornful. But his delight is in the Law of the Lord, and in His Law doth he meditate day and night. And he shall be like a tree planted by the rivers of water, that bringeth forth his fruit in his season; his leaf also shall not wither; and whatsoever he doeth shall prosper.

The ungodly are not so, but are like the chaff which the wind driveth away. Therefore the ungodly shall not stand in the Judgment, nor sinners in the congregation of the righteous. For the Lord knoweth the way of the righteous; but the way of the ungodly shall perish.

# The Morning Prayer

GOD, whose mercies are new every morning, we beseech Thee to bless our home with Thy peace, which passes all the understanding of the natural heart of man. Grant us an abundant measure of Thy grace, that our household may be filled with contentment and kindness. Not only for our own family do we plead, but for the homes of all Thy children.

Wherever troubled hearts are longing for peace, perplexed souls doubt Thy mercies, hungry men and women are asking for bread, the sick and the suffering seeking relief, come to them in Thy love, and reveal Thyself to them as a very present Help in all troubles of life.

In Thy loving-kindness cleanse us all through the precious blood of Christ, our Savior, and keep us in Thy grace and steadfast in faith.

As we are about to go to our daily tasks, bless Thou the labors of our hands and direct our every thought as we plan and perform the duties which are assigned to us. Graciously protect all the children as they go to school or to their play. Bless all little babes. Watch over the sick and those who wait on them in the long hours of anxiety. This we ask in Jesus' name. Amen.

## THE MORNING HYMN

Blessed are the sons of God,
They are bought with Christ's own blood;
They are ransomed from the grave,
Life eternal they shall have:
With them numbered may we be
Here and in eternity!

They are justified by grace,
They enjoy the Savior's peace;
All their sins are washed away,
They shall stand in God's great Day:
With them numbered may we be
Here and in eternity!

They are lights upon the earth,
Children of a heavenly birth;
One with God, with Jesus one,
Glory is in them begun:
With them numbered may we be
Here and in eternity! Amen.

# Monday Evening

## Psalm 32

BLESSED is he whose transgression is forgiven, whose sin is covered. Blessed is the man unto whom the Lord imputeth not iniquity and in whose spirit there is no guile; when I kept silence, my bones waxed old through my roaring all the day long. For day and night Thy hand was heavy upon me; my moisture is turned into the drought of summer. Selah. I acknowledged my sin unto Thee, and mine iniquity have I not hid. I said, I will confess my transgressions unto the Lord; and Thou forgavest the iniquity of my sin. Selah. For this shall every one that is godly pray unto Thee in a time when Thou mayest be found. Surely in the floods of great waters they shall not come nigh unto him.

Thou art my Hiding Place; Thou shalt preserve me from trouble; Thou shalt compass me about with songs of deliverance. Selah.

I will instruct thee and teach thee in the way which thou shalt go; I will guide thee with mine eye.

Be ye not as the horse or as the mule, which have no understanding; whose mouth must be held in with bit and bridle lest they come near unto thee.

Many sorrows shall be to the wicked; but he that trusteth in the Lord, mercy shall compass him about.

Be glad in the Lord and rejoice, ye righteous; and shout for joy, all ye that are upright in heart.

# The Evening Prayer

GRACIOUS and divine Lord, we know that Thou dost not count our sins against us nor cast us away from Thy presence as long as we hide in the sacred wounds of Thy Son, Jesus Christ, our Lord. We acknowledge in this evening hour our many transgressions and confess that we have not done Thy will at all times nor fulfilled Thy holy commandments. Forgive us and let us dwell in peace in this coming night.

Remove from our hearts all envy, strife, contention. Forgiven by Thee, may we be forgiving and thoughtful. Let the fruits of Thy Holy Spirit enrich our lives with the graces of contentment, joy, hope, and love.

Lord, we ask Thee to bless all the homes of the nation with peace. Wherever there are misunderstandings, contentions, bitterness, and strife, let Thy Word enter in to reconcile those hearts which are estranged one from another.

Above all, we pray Thee, heavenly Father, to rule and to direct all things in our homes and lives through Thy Word, that we may live at peace with Thee and with one another and find our greatest joy in Christ Jesus, our Redeemer. Amen.

## THE EVENING HYMN

My hope is built on nothing less
Than Jesus' blood and righteousness;
I dare not trust the sweetest frame,
But wholly lean on Jesus' name.
On Christ, the solid Rock, I stand;
All other ground is sinking sand.

When darkness veils His lovely face,
I rest on His unchanging grace;
In every high and stormy gale
My anchor holds within the veil.
On Christ, the solid Rock, I stand;
All other ground is sinking sand.

When He shall come with trumpet sound,
Oh, may I then in Him be found,
Clothed in His righteousness alone,
Faultless to stand before the throne!
On Christ, the solid Rock, I stand;
All other ground is sinking sand. Amen.

# Tuesday Morning

## Philippians 4

BE careful [overanxious] for nothing; but in everything by prayer and supplication, with thanksgiving, let your requests be made known unto God. And the peace of God, which passeth all understanding, shall keep your hearts and minds through Christ Jesus.

Finally, brethren, whatsoever things are true, whatsoever things are honest, whatsoever things are just, whatsoever things are pure, whatsoever things are lovely, whatsoever things are of good report; if there be any virtue, and if there be any praise, think on these things.

Those things, which ye have both learned, and received, and heard, and seen in me, do; and the God of peace shall be with you. But

I rejoiced in the Lord greatly that now at the
last your care of me hath flourished again;
wherein ye were also careful, but ye lacked
opportunity. Not that I speak in respect of
want; for I have learned in whatsoever state
I am therewith to be content. I know both
how to be abased, and I know how to abound;
everywhere and in all things I am instructed
both to be full and to be hungry, both to
abound and to suffer need. I can do all things
through Christ, which strengtheneth me.

# The Morning Prayer

LORD JESUS, Savior of my soul, abide
with us throughout this day of grace.
Thy power must sustain us, Thy mercy forgive us our sins, and Thy love lead us into
those paths acceptable to Thee. Thy Word
is the guide of our day and the light by
which we know the way. Reveal Thyself in

a greater measure to us who trust in Thee as sheep of Thy fold.

Bless our home with Thy continuous presence, and remove from our hearts all anxiety and fear. Come Thou with healing to each troubled soul, and comfort those who sorrow and all who are perplexed. Give to us contented hearts and untroubled minds, that we may say with trusting hearts this day: Thy will be done, and then know that Thy will is a good and gracious will.

Strengthen our faith, and keep us steadfast in Thy Word until we shall stand in Thy glorious presence to worship Thee world without end. Amen.

## THE MORNING HYMN

Savior, I follow on,
  Guided by Thee,
Seeing not yet the hand
  That leadeth me.
Hushed be my heart and still,
Fear I no further ill,
Only to meet Thy will
  My will shall be.

Riven the rock for me
  Thirst to relieve,
Manna from heaven falls
  Fresh every eve;
Never a want severe
Causeth my eye a tear
But Thou dost whisper near,
  "Only believe."

Savior, I long to walk
  Closer with Thee;
Led by Thy guiding hand,
  Ever to be
Constantly near Thy side,
Quickened and purified,
Living for Him who died
  Freely for me. Amen.

# Tuesday Evening

## Psalm 90

L ORD, Thou has been our Dwelling Place in all generations. Before the mountains were brought forth or ever Thou hadst formed the earth and the world, even from everlasting to everlasting, Thou art God.

Thou turnest man to destruction and sayest, Return, ye children of men. For a thousand years in Thy sight are but as yesterday when it is past and as a watch in the night. Thou carriest them away as with a flood; they are as a sleep; in the morning they are like grass which groweth up. In the morning it flourisheth and groweth up; in the evening it is cut down and withereth. For we are consumed by Thine anger, and by Thy wrath are we troubled. Thou hast set our iniquities before Thee, our secret sins in the light of Thy countenance. For all our days are passed away in Thy wrath; we spend our years as a tale that is told. The days of our years are threescore years and ten; and if by reason of strength they be fourscore years, yet is their strength labor and sorrow; for it is soon cut off, and we fly away. Who knoweth the power of Thine anger? Even according to Thy fear, so is Thy wrath. So teach us to number our days that we may apply our hearts unto wisdom.

Return, O Lord; how long? And let it repent Thee concerning Thy servants. Oh, satisfy us early with Thy mercy that we may rejoice and be glad all our days. Make us glad according to the days wherein Thou hast afflicted us, and the years wherein we have seen evil. Let Thy work appear unto Thy servants and Thy glory unto their children. And let the beauty of the Lord, our God, be upon us; and establish Thou the work of our hands upon us; yea, the work of our hands establish Thou it.

# The Evening Prayer

O GOD, Thou art our God from everlasting to everlasting, the great I AM of eternity, loving us in Christ Jesus, whom Thou hast sent for our redemption into the world of sin. Forgive all sins and the many transgressions of those who seek Thee in mercy. Graciously blot out all our trespasses, and preserve us in Thy grace from day to day.

Dwell in our homes and hearts, and direct our steps that we may do those things which are pleasing to Thee and glorify Thy holy name. Protect us with the covert of Thy wings.

Teach us daily through Thy Word, and grant that we may apply its instructions to our lives and gladly serve Thee throughout the days of our sojourn here on earth.

Lighten our burdens, fill our hearts with contentment, and bless us with a restful sleep. Into Thy hands of mercy and good-

ness we place ourselves and those whom we
love, asking for protection and guidance and
life eternal. In Jesus' name we ask this of
Thee, most gracious Father in heaven. Amen.

## THE EVENING HYMN

Jesus, Savior, pilot me
Over life's tempestuous sea;
Unknown waves before me roll,
Hiding rock and treacherous shoal.
Chart and compass come from Thee:
Jesus, Savior, pilot me.

As a mother stills her child,
Thou canst hush the ocean wild;
Boisterous waves obey Thy will
When Thou say'st to them, "Be still!"
Wondrous Sovereign of the sea,
Jesus, Savior, pilot me.

When at last I near the shore
And the fearful breakers roar
'Twixt me and the peaceful rest,
Then, while leaning on Thy breast,
May I hear Thee say to me,
"Fear not, I will pilot thee."

# Wednesday Morning

## Psalm 46

GOD is our Refuge and Strength, a very present Help in trouble. Therefore will not we fear, though the earth be removed and though the mountains be carried into the midst of the sea, though the waters thereof roar and be troubled, though the mountains shake with the swelling thereof. Selah.

There is a river the streams whereof shall make glad the city of God, the holy place of the tabernacles of the Most High. God is in the midst of her; she shall not be moved; God shall help her, and that right early. The heathen raged, the kingdoms were moved; He uttered His voice, the earth melted. The Lord of hosts is with us; the God of Jacob is our Refuge. Selah.

Come, behold the works of the Lord, what desolations He hath made in the earth.

He maketh wars to cease unto the end of the earth; He breaketh the bow and cutteth the spear in sunder; He burneth the chariot in the fire.

Be still, and know that I am God. I will be exalted among the heathen; I will be exalted in the earth. The Lord of hosts is with us; the God of Jacob is our refuge. Selah.

# The Morning Prayer

GOD, Thou hast been our Help in the yesteryears, forgiving sin and blotting out transgressions. Be Thou our Stay and Strength in the days which are before us, and carry us safely through the dangers which beset us. Show us Thy salvation from day to day. Without Thee life would be hopeless and death terrifying. But in Christ Jesus Thou art our reconciled Father, our Refuge in trouble, our Strength in temptation, and our Guide and Deliverer as we pass through the valley of death.

We thank Thee for the gift of Thy Son, our Lord, in whom we have salvation. We praise Thee for the revelation of Thy Gospel, which gives us the blessed assurance of the resurrection unto life eternal. Grant us grace to hold fast to Thy promises and daily to find peace, joy, contentment, in Thee and protection for the day. Forgive us wherever we have offended Thee, and blot out all our sins through Jesus Christ, the Savior of us all. Amen.

## THE MORNING HYMN

A mighty Fortress is our God,
  A trusty Shield and Weapon;
He helps us free from every need
  That hath us now o'ertaken.
The old evil Foe
Now means deadly woe;
Deep guile and great might
Are His dread arms in fight,
  On earth is not his equal.

With might of ours can naught be done,
  Soon were our loss effected;
But for us fights the Valiant One,
  Whom God Himself elected.
Ask ye, Who is this?
Jesus Christ it is,
Of Sabaoth Lord,
And there's none other God;
  He holds the field forever.

Though devils all the world should fill,
  All eager to devour us,
We tremble not, we fear no ill,
  They shall not overpower us.
This world's prince may still
Scowl fierce as he will,
He can harm us none,
He's judged; the deed is done;
  One little word can fell him.

The Word they still shall let remain
  Nor any thanks have for it;
He's by our side upon the plain
  With His good gifts and Spirit.
And take they our life,
Goods, fame, child, and wife,
Let these all be gone,
They yet have nothing won;
  The Kingdom ours remaineth.
                    Amen.

# Wednesday Evening

## Romans 8

LIKEWISE the Spirit also helpeth our infirmities; for we know not what we should pray for as we ought; but the Spirit itself maketh intercession for us with groanings which cannot be uttered. And He that searcheth the hearts knoweth what is the mind of the Spirit, because He maketh intercession for the saints according to the will of God. And we know that all things work together for good to them that love God, to them who are the called according to His purpose. For whom He did foreknow He also did predestinate to be conformed to the image of His Son, that He might be the First-born among many brethren. Moreover, whom He did predestinate, them He also called; and whom He called, them He also justified; and whom He justified, them He also glorified.

What shall we then say to these things? If God be for us, who can be against us? He that spared not His own Son, but delivered Him up for us all, how shall He not with Him also freely give us all things? Who shall lay anything to the charge of God's elect? It is God that justifieth. Who is he that condemneth? It is Christ that died, yea rather, that is risen again, who is even at the right hand of God, who also maketh intercession for us.

Who shall separate us from the love of Christ? Shall tribulation, or distress, or persecution, or famine, or nakedness, or peril, or sword? As it is written, For Thy sake we are killed all the day long; we are accounted as sheep for the slaughter. Nay, in all these things we are more than conquerors through Him that loved us. For I am persuaded that neither death, nor life, nor angels, nor principalities, nor powers, nor things present, nor things to come, nor height, nor depth, nor any other creature shall be able to separate us from the love of God, which is in Christ Jesus, our Lord.

# The Evening Prayer

LORD GOD eternal, look in favor and love upon us as we come to Thee at the close of another day of grace. Purge us of all our sins and fill our hearts and minds with that peace which gives us assurance of Thy divine love in Christ Jesus, who has given Himself as a Ransom for us all.

Increase in us this saving faith and draw us as a Christian family to Thyself with Thy constraining love. Let nothing take from us the blessed assurance that Thy boundless love in Christ Jesus helps us to the uttermost.

Even in days of trouble, reverses, sickness, and want teach us that all things turn to the good of those who love Thee, even though we look through a glass darkly for the time being. If we doubt Thy mercies and Thy goodness and good will, lead us to the Cross, that we may behold there the outpouring of Thine infinite grace. Let the conviction grow in us that there is nothing in life and death, time and eternity, which can separate us from Thy love which Thou hast shown us in Christ Crucified, who now is our risen and ever living Savior. Amen.

## THE EVENING HYMN

Abide, O dearest Jesus,
   Among us with Thy grace
That Satan may not harm us
   Nor we to sin give place.

Abide, O dear Redeemer,
   Among us with Thy Word,
And thus now and hereafter
   True peace and joy afford.

Abide with Thy protection
   Among us, Lord, our Strength,
Lest world and Satan fell us
   And overcome at length.

Abide, O faithful Savior,
Among us with Thy love;
Grant steadfastness, and help us
To reach our home above. Amen.

# Thursday Morning

## Psalm 139

O LORD, Thou hast searched me and known me. Thou knowest my down-sitting and mine uprising; Thou understandest my thought afar off. Thou compassest my path and my lying down and art acquainted with all my ways. For there is not a word in my tongue but, lo, O Lord, Thou knowest it altogether. Thou hast beset me behind and before and laid Thine hand upon me. Such knowledge is too wonderful for me; it is high, I cannot attain unto it.

Whither shall I go from Thy Spirit? Or whither shall I flee from Thy presence? If I ascend up into heaven, Thou art there; if I make my bed in hell, behold, Thou art there. If I take the wings of the morning and dwell in the uttermost parts of the sea, even there shall Thy hand lead me, and Thy right hand shall hold me. If I say, Surely the darkness shall cover me, even the night shall be light about me. Yea, the darkness hideth not from Thee; but the night shineth as the day; the darkness and the light are both alike to Thee. For Thou hast possessed my reins; Thou hast covered me in my mother's womb. I will praise Thee, for I am fearfully and wonderfully made. Marvelous are Thy works, and that my soul knoweth right well.

How precious also are Thy thoughts unto me, O God! How great is the sum of them! If I should count them, they are more in number than the sand. When I awake, I am still with Thee.

Search me, O God, and know my heart; try me and know my thoughts; and see if there be any wicked way in me, and lead me in the way everlasting.

# The Morning Prayer

WE begin this day in Thy name, Lord God, almighty and most gracious. May each hour be hallowed by Thee, and Thy presence go with us as we leave and as we enter this home. Thou knowest our every word and not even our thoughts can we hide from Thee. Keep them pure and clean and order our steps throughout the day. We acknowledge that Thy goodness gives us bread and Thy mercy forgives all our sins.

Grant that we may perform our many duties acceptably to Thee and assume with cheerful mind each and every responsibility.

Remove from our lives all worries and irritations. Keep us in a hopeful mood. Open our eyes to see opportunities to confess Jesus as our Savior and to serve Him with greater faithfulness. These things we ask of Thee, Thou Searcher of hearts, in the name and for the sake of Jesus Christ, Thy Son. Amen.

## THE MORNING HYMN

Approach, my soul, the Mercy Seat,
  Where Jesus answers prayer;
There humbly fall before His feet,
  For none can perish there.

Thy promise is my only plea,
  With this I venture nigh;
Thou callest burdened souls to Thee,
  And such, O Lord, am I.

Bowed down beneath a load of sin,
  By Satan sorely pressed,
By wars without and fears within,
  I come to Thee for rest.

Be Thou my Shield and Hiding Place,
　That, sheltered near Thy side,
I may my fierce Accuser face
　And tell him Thou hast died.

O wondrous Love, to bleed and die,
　To bear the cross and shame,
That guilty sinners such as I
　Might plead Thy gracious name!
　　　　　　　　　　　　Amen.

# Thursday Evening

## Hebrews 12

LET us run with patience the race that is set before us. Looking unto Jesus, the Author and Finisher of our faith, who for the joy that was set before Him endured the cross, despising the shame, and is set down at the right hand of the throne of God. For consider Him that endured such contradiction of sinners against Himself, lest ye be wearied and faint in your minds.

Ye have not yet resisted unto blood, striving against sin. And ye have forgotten the exhortation which speaketh unto you as unto children, My Son, despise not thou the chastening of the Lord, nor faint when thou art rebuked of Him; for whom the Lord loveth He chasteneth, and scourgeth every son whom He receiveth. If ye endure chastening, God dealeth with you as with sons; for what son is he whom the father chasteneth not? But if ye be without chastisement, whereof all are partakers, then are ye bastards and not sons.

Furthermore, we have had fathers of our flesh which corrected us, and we gave them reverence; shall we not much rather be in subjection unto the Father of spirits and live? For they verily for a few days chastened us after their own pleasure, but He for our profit, that we might be partakers of His holiness.

Now no chastening for the present seemeth to be joyous, but grievous; nevertheless, afterward it yieldeth the peaceable fruit of righteousness unto them which are exercised thereby.

Wherefore lift up the hands which hang down, and the feeble knees, and make straight paths for your feet, lest that which is lame be turned out of the way; but let it rather be healed. Follow peace with all men and holiness, without which no man shall see the Lord.

# The Evening Prayer

WE look to Thee, Lord Jesus, eternal Redeemer of souls, who wast despised and rejected of men and forsaken of Thine own Father because of our transgressions. As we look up to Thee, crucified on the accursed tree, we are mindful of our personal shortcomings and sins. We are ashamed indeed.

Turn not from us, but let Thy loving-kindness blot out every evil which we have done.

As the chastening hand of Thy Father rests upon us, grant us the grace to accept patiently this fatherly correction, knowing that His love is seeking our eternal welfare. Take all rebellion out of our hearts, and teach us to know that His will is wiser than our own.

Let Thy peace rule our hearts and Thy love set aglow in us a deeper devotion and a greater zeal. Make us faithful, and keep us steadfast, glorifying Thy name through our patience, cheerfulness, and contentment of mind. Give us grace and strength to walk daily in newness of life as it becometh Christian people. We ask it in Thy name. Amen and Amen.

## THE EVENING HYMN

In the hour of trial,
  Jesus, plead for me,
Lest by base denial
  I depart from Thee.
When Thou see'st me waver,
  With a look recall
Nor from fear or favor,
  Suffer me to fall.

With forbidden pleasures
  Would this vain world charm
Or its tempting treasures
  Spread to work me harm.
Bring to my remembrance
  Sad Gethsemane
Or, in darker semblance,
  Cross-crowned Calvary.

Should Thy mercy send me
  Sorrow, toil, and woe,
Or should pain attend me
  On my path below,
Grant that I may never
  Fail Thy hand to see;
Grant that I may ever
  Cast my care on Thee.

When my last hour cometh,
    Fraught with strife and pain,
When my dust returneth
    To the dust again,
On Thy truth relying,
    Through that mortal strife,
Jesus, take me, dying,
    To eternal life. Amen.

# Friday Morning

## Psalm 63

O GOD, Thou art my God; early will I seek Thee. My soul thirsteth for Thee, my flesh longeth for Thee, in a dry and thirsty land, where no water is, to see Thy power and Thy glory, so as I have seen Thee in the Sanctuary.

Because Thy loving-kindness is better than life, my lips shall praise Thee. Thus will I bless Thee while I live; I will lift up my hands in Thy name.

My soul shall be satisfied as with marrow and fatness, and my mouth shall praise Thee with joyful lips, when I remember Thee upon my bed and meditate on Thee in the night watches. Because Thou hast been my Help, therefore in the shadow of Thy wings will I rejoice. My soul followeth hard after Thee; Thy right hand upholdeth me.

# The Morning Prayer

O GOD, Thy loving-kindness is as boundless as the sea, and Thy goodness from generation to generation has sustained our family. Our grateful hearts praise Thee.

We cannot but speak of Thy mercies day after day. We stand in awe before Thee. Daily Thou forgivest sin and strengthenest faith through Thy Holy Spirit.

Life would be meaningless if it were not for Thy loving-kindness; life would break if it were not for Thine upholding hand; life would be filled with despondent fear if we could not hide in the shadow of Thy wings. So we come in this morning hour to find protection underneath Thine almighty arms. No one can pluck us out of Thy hands. No harm can come to us as we are sheltered by Thee.

With confidence we go forward for the day, certain that Thou as our heavenly Father in Christ Jesus wilt guide us with Thine eye and be our help in every trouble. Amen.

## THE MORNING HYMN

My faith looks up to Thee,
Thou Lamb of Calvary,
    Savior divine!
Now hear me while I pray;
Take all my guilt away;
Oh, let me from this day
    Be wholly Thine!

May Thy rich grace impart
Strength to my fainting heart,
  My zeal inspire.
As Thou hast died for me,
Oh, may my love to Thee
Pure, warm, and changeless be,
  A living fire!

While life's dark maze I tread
And griefs around me spread,
  Be Thou my Guide.
Bid darkness turn to day,
Wipe sorrow's tears away,
Nor let me ever stray
  From Thee aside.

When ends life's transient dream,
When death's cold, sullen stream
  Shall o'er me roll,
Blest Savior, then, in love,
Fear and distrust remove;
Oh, bear me safe above,
  A ransomed soul!  Amen.

# 𝔉riday 𝔈bening

## Isaiah 40

COMFORT ye, comfort ye My people, saith your God. Speak ye comfortably to Jerusalem, and cry unto her that her warfare is accomplished, that her iniquity is pardoned; for she hath received of the Lord's hand double for all her sins.

The voice of him that crieth in the wilderness, Prepare ye the way of the Lord, make straight in the desert a highway for our God. Every valley shall be exalted, and every mountain and hill shall be made low, and the crooked shall be made straight, and the rough places plain; and the glory of the Lord shall be revealed, and all flesh shall see it together; for the mouth of the Lord hath spoken it.

The voice said, Cry. And he said, What shall I cry? All flesh is grass, and all the goodliness thereof is as the flower of the field. The grass withereth, the flower fadeth, because the Spirit of the Lord bloweth upon it; surely the people is grass. The grass withereth, the flower fadeth; but the Word of our God shall stand forever.

O Zion, that bringest good tidings, get thee up into the high mountain. O Jerusalem, that bringest good tidings, lift up thy voice with strength; lift it up, be not afraid; say unto the cities of Judah, Behold your God! Behold, the Lord God will come with strong hand, and His arm shall rule for Him. Behold, His reward is with Him, and His work before Him. He shall feed His flock like a shepherd; He shall gather the lambs with His arm, and carry them in His bosom, and shall gently lead those that are with young.

Hast thou not known, hast thou not heard, that the everlasting God, the Lord, the Creator of the ends of the earth, fainteth not, neither is weary? There is no searching of His understanding. He giveth power to the faint, and to them that have no might He increaseth strength. Even the youths shall faint and be weary, and the young men shall utterly fall; but they that wait upon the Lord shall renew their strength; they shall mount up with wings as eagles; they shall run and not be weary; and they shall walk and not faint.

# The Evening Prayer

HEAVENLY FATHER, gracious and merciful in Christ Jesus, comfort us with the blessed assurance of the forgiveness of all our sins. As we go into the night, seeking rest from the tasks and duties of the day, let no unforgiven sin haunt us nor cling to us. We depend upon Thee for protection. We place ourselves into Thy hands for safe-keeping.

Watch over all Thy children. Comfort the sorrowing. Give strength to the weary. Remove worrisome thoughts from our minds, knowing that Thou sittest upon the circle of the earth, never failing those who put their trust in Thee.

Amid the uncertainties of life lead us into Thy Word, and strengthen our faith through Thy promises. Then shall Thy glory be revealed, and our hearts shall praise Thee who hast made us Thine through Jesus Christ, our Savior. Amen.

## THE EVENING HYMN

Rock of Ages, cleft for me,
Let me hide myself in Thee;
Let the water and the blood
From Thy riven side which flowed
Be of sin the double cure,
Cleanse me from its guilt and power.

Not the labors of my hands
Can fulfill Thy Law's demands;
Could my zeal no respite know,
Could my tears forever flow,
All for sin could not atone;
Thou must save, and Thou alone.

Nothing in my hand I bring,
Simply to Thy Cross I cling;
Naked, come to Thee for dress;
Helpless, look to Thee for grace;
Foul, I to the fountain fly—
Wash me, Savior, or I die!

While I draw this fleeting breath,
When my eyelids close in death,
When I soar to worlds unknown,
See Thee on Thy judgment throne,
Rock of Ages, cleft for me,
Let me hide myself in Thee! Amen.

# Saturday Morning

## Psalm 51

HAVE mercy upon me, O God, according to Thy loving-kindness; according unto the multitude of Thy tender mercies blot out my transgressions. Wash me thoroughly from mine iniquity, and cleanse me from my sin. For I acknowledge my transgressions, and my sin is ever before me. Against Thee, Thee only, have I sinned and done this evil in Thy sight; that Thou mightest be justified when Thou speakest, and be clear when Thou judgest. Behold, I was shapen in iniquity, and in sin did my mother conceive me. Behold, Thou desirest truth in the inward parts: and in the hidden part Thou shalt make me to know wisdom. Purge me with hyssop, and I shall be clean; wash me, and I shall be whiter than snow. Make me to hear joy and gladness, that the bones which Thou hast broken may rejoice. Hide Thy face from my sins, and blot out all mine iniquities.

Create in me a clean heart, O God, and renew a right spirit within me. Cast me not away from Thy presence, and take not Thy Holy Spirit from me. Restore unto me the joy of Thy salvation, and uphold me with Thy free spirit. Then will I teach transgressors Thy ways, and sinners shall be converted unto Thee. Deliver me from blood-guiltiness, O God, Thou God of my salvation, and my tongue shall sing aloud of Thy righteousness.

O Lord, open Thou my lips, and my mouth shall show forth Thy praise. For Thou desirest not sacrifice, else would I give it; Thou delightest not in burnt offering. The sacrifices of God are a broken spirit; a broken and a contrite heart, O God, Thou wilt not despise.

# The Morning Prayer

HAVE mercy, O God, have mercy upon us, and accept us for Jesus' sake, and preserve us in Thy grace. Only then shall our hearts be filled with peace and our day with joy. Help us to face the vexing problems, and remove the many irritations which so easily upset us.

Let Thy Holy Spirit guide and direct us into paths pleasing to Thee, and open Thou our lips to praise Thee, who so graciously hast sent Thy Son into the world to blot out the multitude of our sins. Cleanse our hearts, and purify our thoughts, and wash clean our hands. Grant that our lives may glorify Thy holy name.

Guard and protect us from the guiles of Satan. Fill us with the joy of salvation that we may go through the day singing Thy praises, who madest us precious in Thy sight through Jesus Christ, whom Thou hast sent into the world as the Savior of us all. Amen.

## THE MORNING HYMN

Come, ye disconsolate, where'er ye languish;
Come to the Mercy Seat, fervently kneel.
Here bring your wounded hearts, here tell
    your anguish;
    Earth has no sorrow that Heaven cannot
    heal.

Joy of the desolate, Light of the straying,
    Hope of the penitent, fadeless and pure;
Here speaks the Comforter, tenderly saying,
    Earth has no sorrow that Heaven cannot
    cure.

Here see the Bread of Life; see waters flowing
    Forth from the throne of God, pure from
    above.
Come to the feast of love; come, ever knowing
    Earth has no sorrow but Heaven can
    remove. Amen.

# Saturday Evening

## Psalm 121

I WILL lift up mine eyes unto the hills from whence cometh my help. My help cometh from the Lord, which made heaven and earth. He will not suffer thy foot to be moved; He that keepeth thee will not slumber. Behold, He that keepeth Israel shall neither slumber nor sleep.

The Lord is thy Keeper; the Lord is thy Shade upon thy right hand. The sun shall not smite thee by day, nor the moon by night. The Lord shall preserve thee from all evil; He shall preserve thy soul. The Lord shall preserve thy going out and thy coming in from this time forth and even forevermore.

# The Evening Prayer

TO THEE we turn, O Lord, in this evening hour to receive Thy divine benediction. Because Thou dost not slumber nor sleep, we can lie down in peace, knowing that Thou wilt protect us, as the Lover of our souls and the Keeper of our lives.

Prepare our hearts to receive Thy Word this coming day, that we may grow in grace and knowledge of Thy Son, who has redeemed us with His own blood. Grant that pastors and people in all Christian churches may exalt the name of Jesus, who is our only Savior. Turn the feet of many people to Thy tabernacles of grace. Grant to every minister of Thy Word power from Thy Holy Spirit to proclaim nothing but the crucified Christ, who is the one hope of a sin-ridden world.

Preserve our going out and our coming in day after day until we shall stand before the throne of the Lamb to praise Him who has washed and cleansed us from all sin and made us kings and priests with Himself in that eternal life in heaven. Amen.

## THE EVENING HYMN

If thou but suffer God to guide thee
    And hope in Him through all thy ways,
He'll give thee strength, whate'er betide thee,
    And bear thee through the evil days.
Who trusts in God's unchanging love
Builds on the rock that naught can move.

What can these anxious cares avail thee,
    These never-ceasing moans and sighs?
What can it help if thou bewail thee
    O'er each dark moment as it flies?
Our cross and trials do but press
The heavier for our bitterness.

Be patient and await His leisure
    In cheerful hope, with heart content
To take whate'er thy Father's pleasure
    And His discerning love hath sent,
Nor doubt our inmost wants are known
To Him who chose us for His own. Amen.

# Treasures of Hope

# THE SECOND WEEK

# THE SECOND WEEK

## Sunday Morning

## Psalm 100

MAKE a joyful noise unto the Lord, all ye lands. Serve the Lord with gladness; come before His presence with singing. Know ye that the Lord, He is God. It is He that hath made us, and not we ourselves; we are His people and the sheep of His pasture. Enter into His gates with thanksgiving, and into His courts with praise; be thankful unto Him, and bless His name. For the Lord is good; His mercy is everlasting; and His truth endureth to all generations.

# The Morning Prayer

DIVINE and gracious Savior, in whose presence we find peace and whose promises bring hope into our lives, look upon us with Thy favor and grace, and open our hearts and ears to receive Thy Word with gladness. We worship and adore Thee as our risen Savior and glorious Redeemer, who through Thy death and resurrection hast prepared for us a place in the eternal mansions.

Some of Thy children, coming before Thee, are weary of the struggle, confused by doubts, perplexed by worries, and heartsick because of their sins. But we all come to Thee as our only Refuge in the day of trouble. Thou alone canst forgive us our trespasses and fill our hearts with peace and joy. Grant that we may appreciate Thy Word, love it, believe it, and follow it.

May this Lord's day be rich in blessings to us and to ten thousands of Thy people; then Thine shall be the glory, Thine the praise, ages upon ages, as our Lord and Savior. Amen.

## THE MORNING HYMN

Almighty God, Thy Word is cast
　　Like seed into the ground;
Now let the dew of heaven descend
　　And righteous fruits abound.

Let not the foe of Christ and man
　　This holy seed remove,
But give it root in every heart
　　To bring forth fruits of love.

Let not the world's deceitful cares
　　The rising plant destroy,
But let it yield a hundredfold
　　The fruits of peace and joy.

Oft as the precious seed is sown,
　　Thy quickening grace bestow,
That all whose souls the truth receive
　　Its saving power may know. Amen.

# 𝔖𝔲𝔫𝔡𝔞𝔶 𝔈𝔳𝔢𝔫𝔦𝔫𝔤

## Psalm 84

HOW amiable are Thy tabernacles, O Lord of hosts! My soul longeth, yea, even fainteth, for the courts of the Lord; my heart and my flesh crieth out for the living God. Yea, the sparrow hath found an house and the swallow a nest for herself, where she may lay her young, even Thine altars, O Lord of hosts, my King and my God.

Blessed are they that dwell in Thy house; they will be still praising Thee. Selah. Blessed is the man whose strength is in Thee, in whose heart are the ways of them. Who passing through the Valley of Baca, make it a well; the rain also filleth the pools. They go from strength to strength; every one of them in Zion appeareth before God.

O Lord God of hosts, hear my prayer; give ear, O God of Jacob. Selah. Behold, O God, our Shield, and look upon the face of Thine anointed. For a day in Thy courts is better than a thousand. I had rather be a doorkeeper in the house of my God than to dwell in the tents of wickedness. For the Lord God is a Sun and Shield; the Lord will give grace and glory. No good thing will He withhold from them that walk uprightly. O Lord of hosts, blessed is the man that trusteth in Thee.

# The Evening Prayer

OH, that we were as wise as the sparrow and as trusting as the swallow, O Lord, our King and our God! Thou hast reared for us an altar on Calvary that we might hide in the sacred wounds of our Redeemer. Grant us the grace to come daily to this place of refuge and find healing from sin and reconciliation and peace with Thee. We thank Thee, merciful Lord, that Thou hast given us Thy Word to strengthen our faith and to nourish our souls. We praise Thee, who hast called us into the kingdom of Thy Son, and we beseech Thee to keep us faithful unto the end of days.

Guide and direct our every step in this new week of grace, that we may by word and deed give honor to Thee, the Father of our Lord Jesus Christ. Dwell Thou with us and bless us with peace, joy, contentment, and patience. We ask this in Jesus' name. Amen.

## THE EVENING HYMN

Beautiful Savior,
King of Creation,
Son of God and Son of Man!
Truly I'd love Thee,
Truly I'd serve Thee,
Light of my soul, my Joy, my Crown.

Fair are the meadows,
Fair are the woodlands,
Robed in flowers of blooming spring;
Jesus is fairer,
Jesus is purer;
He makes our sorrowing spirit sing.

Fair is the sunshine,
Fair is the moonlight,
Bright the sparkling stars on high;
Jesus shines brighter,
Jesus shines purer,
Than all the angels in the sky.

Beautiful Savior,
Lord of the nations,
Son of God and Son of Man!
Glory and honor,
Praise, adoration,
Now and forevermore be Thine!
                              Amen.

# Monday Morning
## Psalm 103

BLESS the Lord, O my soul; and, all that is within me, bless His holy name. Bless the Lord, O my soul, and forget not all His benefits; who forgiveth all thine iniquities, who healeth all thy diseases, who redeemeth thy life from destruction, who crowneth thee with loving-kindness and tender mercies, who satisfieth thy mouth with good things, so that thy youth is renewed like the eagle's.

The Lord executeth righteousness and judgment for all that are oppressed. He made known His ways unto Moses, His acts unto the children of Israel. The Lord is merciful and gracious, slow to anger, and plenteous in mercy. He will not always chide, neither will He keep His anger forever. He hath not dealt with us after our sins nor rewarded us according to our iniquities. For as the heaven is high above the earth, so great is His mercy toward them that fear Him. As far as the east is from the west, so far hath He removed our transgressions from us. Like as a father pitieth his children, so the Lord pitieth them that fear Him. For He knoweth our frame; He remembereth that we are dust.

As for man, his days are as grass; as a flower of the field, so he flourisheth. For the wind passeth over it, and it is gone; and the place thereof shall know it no more. But the mercy of the Lord is from everlasting to everlasting upon them that fear Him, and His righteousness unto children's children, to such as keep His covenant, and to those that remember His commandments to do them.

The Lord hath prepared His throne in the heavens, and His kingdom ruleth over all. Bless the Lord, ye His angels, that excel in strength, that do His commandments, hearkening unto the voice of His word. Bless ye the Lord, all ye His hosts, ye ministers of His that do His pleasure. Bless the Lord, all His works, in all places of His dominion; bless the Lord, O my soul.

# The Morning Prayer

MORNING, noon, and night we praise Thee, O Lord, who art our God from everlasting and our Father in Christ Jesus. Thy mercies are as boundless as the sea, and Thy loving-kindness reaches down to every sinful heart. Grant us all cleansing and fill us with Thy divine peace.

Lord, we are not worthy of Thy manifold blessings, so graciously given; yet our hearts rejoice as Thou dost abundantly pardon us in Christ Jesus. We praise Thee as Thou openest Thy hand to supply every need of our present life. Remembering Thy loving-kindness in the past, we go forth into the day with greater certainty, less anxiety, and firmer confidence. We are sure of Thy guidance. Give us grace to trust in Thee at all times as our heavenly Father through the merits of Jesus Christ, our Lord and our Savior. Amen.

## THE MORNING HYMN

Awake, my soul, to joyful lays
And sing Thy great Redeemer's praise —
He justly claims a song from me —
His loving-kindness, oh, how free!

He saw me ruined in the Fall,
Yet loved me notwithstanding all.
He saved me from my lost estate
His loving-kindness, oh, how great!

When I was Satan's easy prey
And deep in debt and bondage lay,
He paid His life for my discharge —
His loving-kindness, oh, how large!

When earthly friends forsake me quite
And I have neither skill nor might,
He's sure my Helper to appear —
His loving-kindness, oh, how near!

Too oft I feel my sinful heart
Prone from my Jesus to depart;
But though I have Him oft forgot,
His loving-kindness changes not. Amen.

# Monday Evening

## Ephesians 2

GOD, who is rich in mercy, for His great
love wherewith He loved us, even when
we were dead in sins, hath quickened us
together with Christ (by grace ye are saved),
and hath raised us up together, and made
us sit together in heavenly places in Christ
Jesus, that in the ages to come He might
show the exceeding riches of His grace in
His kindness toward us through Christ Jesus.

For by grace are ye saved through faith;
and that not of yourselves; it is the gift of
God; not of works, lest any man should
boast. For we are His workmanship, created

in Christ Jesus unto good works, which God hath before ordained that we should walk in them.

Wherefore remember that ye, being in time past Gentiles in the flesh, who are called uncircumcision by that which is called the circumcision in the flesh made by hands, that at that time ye were without Christ, being aliens from the commonwealth of Israel, and strangers from the covenants of promise, having no hope, and without God in the world; but now in Christ Jesus ye, who sometimes were far off, are made nigh by the blood of Christ. For He is our Peace.

# The Evening Prayer

WITH grateful hearts we approach Thy throne of grace, most merciful God, giving thanks to Thee, who hast raised us from our spiritual death to live in the presence of Thy Son, Jesus Christ, our Lord.

We rejoice to dwell in Thy household with all fellow citizens and all the saints of the ages. Only Thy grace could transform our hearts; only Thy power could make us new creatures.

We rejoice in the hope and the peace which is ours through the blood of Thy Son. Grant that we may always appreciate the riches of Thy mercy and Thy loving-kindness toward us, who without Christ would be aliens and foreigners, lost and condemned.

Let Thy Word dwell in our midst richly, and let Christ rule our hearts and Thy Holy Spirit build in us daily a temple fit as Thine eternal dwelling place. We bring these petitions to Thee through Jesus Christ, our Savior. Amen.

## THE EVENING HYMN

Let me be Thine forever,
  Thou faithful God and Lord;
Let me forsake Thee never
  Nor wander from Thy Word.
Lord, do not let me waver,
  But give me steadfastness,
And for such grace forever
  Thy holy name I'll bless.

Lord Jesus, my Salvation,
  My Light, my Life divine,
My only Consolation,
  Oh, make me wholly Thine!
For Thou hast dearly bought me
  With blood and bitter pain.
Let me, since Thou has sought me,
  Eternal life obtain.

And Thou, O Holy Spirit,
  My Comforter and Guide,
Grant that in Jesus' merit
  I always may confide,
Him to the end confessing
  Whom I have known by faith.
Give me Thy constant blessing
  And grant a Christian death.
                    Amen.

# Tuesday Morning

## John 15

I AM the true Vine, and My Father is the Husbandman. Every branch in Me that beareth not fruit He taketh away; and every branch that beareth fruit, He purgeth it that it may bring forth more fruit. Now ye are clean through the Word which I have spoken unto you. Abide in Me, and I in you. As the branch cannot bear fruit of itself except it abide in the vine, no more can ye except ye abide in Me. I am the Vine, ye are the branches; he that abideth in Me and I in him, the same bringeth forth much fruit; for without Me ye can do nothing. If a man abide not in Me, he is cast forth as a branch and is withered; and men gather them and cast them into the fire, and they are burned.

If ye abide in Me and My words abide in you, ye shall ask what ye will, and it shall be done unto you. Herein is My Father glorified, that ye bear much fruit; so shall ye be My disciples. As the Father hath loved Me, so have I loved you; continue ye in My love. If ye keep My commandments, ye shall abide in My love, even as I have kept My Father's commandments and abide in His love.

These things have I spoken unto you that My joy might remain in you, and that your joy might be full. This is My commandment, that ye love one another as I have loved you. Greater love hath no man than this, that a man lay down his life for his friends. Ye are My friends if ye do whatsoever I command you. Henceforth I call you not servants; for the servant knoweth not what his lord doeth; but I have called you friends; for all things that I have heard of My Father I have made known unto you. Ye have not chosen Me, but I have chosen you, and ordained you that ye should go and bring forth fruit, and that your fruit should remain, that whatsoever ye shall ask of the Father in My name He may give it you.

# The Morning Prayer

LORD JESUS, the very best of friends, we rejoice to know that Thou hast called us Thine own and revealed to us all the truths we need to know for our eternal salvation. In Thy friendship is joy, and in Thy love is everlasting life. Abide with us as we go forth from this home and grant that we may in word and conduct bear witness to Thee who hast chosen us as Thine own. Greater love has no one shown to us, for Thou hast given Thy life for our redemption. Grant that Thy sacrifice on Calvary constrain us to be more forgiving, richer in good works, and more diligent in prayer.

Forgive us our many shortcomings, and draw us closer to Thyself, that through Thy continued and abiding presence we may be able to bring forth more fruits of Christian faith. Go with us as we perform our daily tasks and bless the labors of our hands. Give us grace to continue in Thy love and remain steadfast in faith unto the end of days. Hear our prayers, Savior and Friend. Amen.

## THE MORNING HYMN

How sweet the name of Jesus sounds
  In a believer's ear!
It soothes his sorrows, heals his wounds,
  And drives away his fear.

It makes the wounded spirit whole
  And calms the troubled breast;
'Tis manna to the hungry soul
  And to the weary, rest.

Dear name! The Rock on which I build,
  My Shield and Hiding Place;
My never-failing Treasury, filled
  With boundless stores of grace.

By Thee my prayers acceptance gain
  Although with sin defiled.
Satan accuses me in vain,
  And I am owned a child.

Jesus, my Shepherd, Guardian, Friend,
  My Prophet, Priest, and King,
My Lord, my Life, my Way, my End,
  Accept the praise I bring. Amen.

# Tuesday Evening

# Matthew 5

AND seeing the multitudes, He went up into a mountain. And when He was set, His disciples came unto Him. And He opened His mouth and taught them, saying: Blessed are the poor in spirit, for theirs is the kingdom of heaven. Blessed are they that mourn, for they shall be comforted. Blessed are the meek, for they shall inherit the earth. Blessed are they which do hunger and thirst after righteousness, for they shall be filled. Blessed are the merciful, for they shall obtain mercy. Blessed are the pure in heart, for they shall see God. Blessed are the peacemakers, for they shall be called the children of God. Blessed are they which are persecuted for righteousness' sake, for theirs is the kingdom of heaven. Blessed are ye when men shall revile you and persecute you and shall say all manner of evil against you falsely for my sake. Rejoice, and be exceeding glad; for great is your reward in heaven; for so persecuted they the prophets which were before you.

Ye are the salt of the earth. But if the salt have lost his savor, wherewith shall it be salted? It is thenceforth good for nothing but to be cast out and to be trodden under foot of men.

Ye are the light of the world. A city that is set on a hill cannot be hid. Neither do men light a candle and put it under a bushel, but on a candlestick, and it giveth light unto all that are in the house. Let your light so shine before men that they may see your good works and glorify your Father which is in heaven.

# The Evening Prayer

SHEPHERD of my soul, lead and guide us safely through this troubled world, and keep us this coming night from every harm and danger. Thou knowest how thankless and helpless we are. In our own strength we cannot withstand storms and fires, sickness and death. However, we can sleep tonight because Thou art with us. Help us to overcome all doubts and misgivings, and let Thy promises strengthen our faith and Thy Gospel heal our souls.

Forgive us all our sins, for which Thou hast died on the Cross. Let us find lasting peace and joy in knowing that Thou dost abundantly pardon. Take every irritation out of our home and hearts.

Make us a praying people, who turn to Thee every hour of the day. Bless the sick with Thy healing, comfort those who mourn, and give strength to the discouraged, and understanding to those who doubt Thy Word. Fill our hearts with the joy of salvation, and shepherd us until life's journey ends. Hear Thou the prayer of Thy people, most adorable Savior. Amen.

## THE EVENING HYMN

Savior, Thy dying love
  Thou gavest me;
Nor should I aught withhold,
  Dear Lord, from Thee.
In love my soul would bow,
My heart fulfill its vow,
Some offering bring Thee now,
  Something for Thee.

O'er the blest Mercy Seat,
  Pleading for me,
My feeble faith looks up,
  Jesus, to Thee.
Help me the cross to bear,
Thy wondrous love declare,
Some song to raise or prayer,
  Something for Thee.

Give me a faithful heart,
　Likeness to Thee,
That each departing day
　Henceforth may see
Some work of love begun,
Some deed of kindness done,
Some wanderer sought and won,
　Something for Thee.

All that I am and have,
　Thy gifts so free,
In joy, in grief, through life,
　Dear Lord, for Thee!
And when Thy face I see,
My ransomed soul shall be
Through all eternity
　Something for Thee. Amen.

# Wednesday Morning

## Psalm 42

A S the hart panteth after the water brooks,
so panteth my soul after Thee, O God.
My soul thirsteth for God, for the living
God. When shall I come and appear before
God? My tears have been my meat day and
night, while they continually say unto me,
Where is thy God? When I remember these
things, I pour out my soul in me; for I had
gone with the multitude, I went with them
to the house of God, with the voice of joy
and praise, with a multitude that kept
holyday.

Why art thou cast down, O my soul,
and why art thou disquieted in me? Hope
thou in God; for I shall yet praise Him for
the help of His countenance.

O my God, my soul is cast down within
me; therefore will I remember Thee from
the land of Jordan, and of the Hermonites,
from the hill Mizar. Deep calleth unto deep
at the noise of Thy waterspouts: all Thy
waves and Thy billows are gone over me.
Yet the Lord will command His loving-kindness in the daytime, and in the night His
song shall be with me, and my prayer unto
the God of my life. I will say unto God, my
Rock, Why hast Thou forgotten me? Why
go I mourning because of the oppression of
the enemy? As with a sword in my bones
mine enemies reproach me, while they say
daily unto me, Where is thy God?

Why art thou cast down, O my soul,
and why art thou disquieted within me?
Hope thou in God; for I shall yet praise Him,
who is the Health of my countenance and
my God.

# The Morning Prayer

GOD eternal and gracious, whose presence means safety, come Thou into our hearts and into our home, and abide with us amid the many perplexities of life. Worried and troubled, we come to Thee, who hast promised to be with us in the hours of trial. Thou hast given us the blessed assurance that Thou wilt forgive in Christ Jesus all our sins and keep us in Thy love and grace.

We are unworthy, we confess, of all these mercies. We have not always loved Thee with all our heart nor placed Thee at all times first in our lives. Other interests have crowded Thee into the shadows; yet Thy covenant gives us the courage to come to Thee and plead for forgiveness and for guidance this day. In Thy mercy keep us steadfast in faith, and in Thy goodness open Thy hands to satisfy us with daily bread.

Remove all perplexing thoughts, and speak peace to our souls, as we lift our hearts and hands in prayer to Thee in the name of Jesus Christ, our eternal Savior. Amen.

## THE MORNING HYMN

As pants the hart for cooling streams
    When heated in the chase,
So longs my soul, O God, for Thee
    And Thy refreshing grace.

For Thee, my God, the living God,
    My thirsty soul doth pine;
Oh, when shall I behold Thy face,
    Thou Majesty Divine?

Why restless, why cast down, my soul?
    Hope still; and thou shalt sing
The praise of Him who is thy God,
    Thy health's eternal Spring.

To Father, Son, and Holy Ghost,
    The God whom we adore,
Be glory as it was, is now,
    And shall be evermore. Amen.

# Wednesday Evening

## Isaiah 53

WHO hath believed our report? And to whom is the arm of the Lord revealed? For He shall grow up before Him as a tender plant, and as a root out of a dry ground. He hath no form nor comeliness; and when we shall see Him, there is no beauty that we should desire Him. He is despised and rejected of men, a man of sorrows and acquainted with grief; and we hid, as it were, our faces from Him. He was despised, and we esteemed Him not.

Surely he hath borne our griefs and carried our sorrows; yet we did esteem Him stricken, smitten of God, and afflicted. But He was wounded for our transgressions; He was bruised for our iniquities; the chastisement of our peace was upon Him; and with His stripes we are healed.

All we, like sheep, have gone astray; we have turned everyone to his own way; and the Lord hath laid on Him the iniquity of us all. He was oppressed, and He was afflicted; yet He opened not His mouth; He is brought as a lamb to the slaughter, and as a sheep before her shearers is dumb, so He openeth not His mouth. He was taken from prison and from judgment, and who shall declare His generation? For He was cut off out of the land of the living; for the transgression of my people was He stricken. And He made His grave with the wicked and with the rich in His death; because He had done no violence, neither was any deceit in His mouth.

Yet it pleased the Lord to bruise Him; He hath put Him to grief. When Thou shalt make His soul an offering for sin, He shall see His seed, He shall prolong His days, and the pleasure of the Lord shall prosper in His hand. He shall see of the travail of His soul and shall be satisfied; by His knowledge shall My righteous Servant justify many; for He shall bear their iniquities. Therefore will I divide Him a portion with the great, and He shall divide the spoil with the strong, because He hath poured out His soul unto death, and He was numbered with the transgressors, and He bare the sin of many and made intercession for the transgressors.

# The Evening Prayer

O CHRIST, Lamb of God, slain for the world's transgressions, we too come to the foot of the Cross, seeking mercy and pardon. Our sins also have nailed Thee to the accursed tree. Our transgressions were Thy burden.

We thank Thee for drinking this bitter cup of redemption that we might be healed. Our grateful hearts have found salvation and hope in Thy words of comfort, in Thy tears of agony, in the work Thou didst finish on Calvary, and in Thy victory over Satan, sin, and death. Daily bring healing to our souls, cleansing to our hearts, and peace to our minds.

Graciously lift us to Thyself, and embrace us with Thy love, and create in us a deeper appreciation of Thy holy Passion.

Today we again dedicate ourselves to Thee, O Christ, and ask Thee to give us strength to serve Thee as Thy faithful disciples. Preserve us in Thy grace until we shall stand in Thy presence to worship Thee world without end as the Lamb once slain but now living in glory, praised and worshiped by the great multitude of heaven. Accept also our adoration. Amen. Hallelujah! Amen.

## THE EVENING HYMN

O sacred Head, now wounded,
  With grief and shame weighed down,
Now scornfully surrounded
  With thorns, Thine only crown.
O sacred Head, what glory,
  What bliss, till now was Thine!
Yet, though despised and gory,
  I joy to call Thee mine.

My burden is Thy Passion,
  Lord, Thou hast borne for me,
For it was my transgression
  Which brought this woe on Thee.
I cast me down before Thee;
  Wrath were my rightful lot.
Have mercy, I implore Thee;
  Redeemer, spurn me not!

Be Thou my Consolation,
  My Shield, when I must die;
Remind me of Thy Passion
  When my last hour draws nigh.
Mine eyes shall then behold Thee,
  Upon Thy cross shall dwell,
My heart by faith enfold Thee.
  Who dieth thus dies well. Amen.

# Thursday Morning

## Psalm 25

UNTO Thee, O Lord, do I lift up my
soul. O my God, I trust in Thee; let
me not be ashamed; let not mine enemies
triumph over me. Yea, let none that wait on
Thee be ashamed; let them be ashamed which
transgress without cause.

Show me Thy ways, O Lord; teach me
Thy paths. Lead me in Thy truth and teach
me, for Thou art the God of my salvation;
on Thee do I wait all the day. Remember, O
Lord, Thy tender mercies and Thy loving-
kindnesses, for they have been ever of old.
Remember not the sins of my youth nor my
transgressions; according to Thy mercy remember Thou me for Thy goodness' sake,
O Lord.

Good and upright is the Lord; therefore
will He teach sinners in the way. The meek

will He guide in judgment, and the meek will He teach His way. All the paths of the Lord are mercy and truth unto such as keep His covenant and His testimonies. For Thy name's sake, O Lord, pardon mine iniquity; for it is great.

What man is he that feareth the Lord? Him shall He teach in the way that he shall choose. His soul shall dwell at ease, and his seed shall inherit the earth. The secret of the Lord is with them that fear Him, and He will show them His covenant.

Mine eyes are ever toward the Lord, for He shall pluck my feet out of the net. Turn Thee unto me, and have mercy upon me, for I am desolate and afflicted. The troubles of my heart are enlarged. O bring Thou me out of my distresses. Look upon mine affliction and my pain, and forgive all my sins. O keep my soul and deliver me; let me not be ashamed; for I put my trust in Thee. Let integrity and uprightness preserve me, for I wait on Thee. Redeem Israel, O God, out of all his troubles.

# The Morning Prayer

TO THEE we come, O Lord, at the beginning of this day, mindful of Thy boundless love, which has reconciled us to Thee through Jesus Christ, our Lord, and made us heirs of life eternal. With grateful hearts we acknowledge Thy goodness and praise Thee, who hast sent Thine only Son to Calvary to redeem us from sin and death. Forgive us all our thoughtlessness, and make us evermore appreciative as we count the many blessings which we so undeservedly receive from Thy bountiful hand. Remove from our hearts and minds all anxious thoughts, and take us safely through this present day. As we go to and fro, protect us with Thine almighty arm.

Let Thy presence fill our household with joy and peace, cheerfulness and hope. Bless our nation with many Christian homes and our country with many God-fearing people; then Thine shall be the glory and the praise, rising from our grateful hearts every hour of the day through Jesus Christ, our Lord. Amen.

## THE MORNING HYMN

Come, follow Me, the Savior spake,
　All in My way abiding;
Deny yourselves, the world forsake,
　Obey My call and guiding;
Oh, bear the cross, whate'er betide,
Take My example for your guide.

I am the Light, I light the way,
　A godly life displaying;
I bid you walk as in the day,
　I keep your feet from straying.
I am the Way, and well I show
How men should sojourn here below.

I teach you how to shun and flee
    What harms your soul's salvation,
Your heart from every guile to free
    From sin and its temptation.
I am the Refuge of the soul
And lead you to your heavenly goal.
Amen.

# Thursday Evening

## Psalm 130

OUT of the depths have I cried unto Thee, O Lord. Lord, hear my voice; let Thine ears be attentive to the voice of my supplications. If Thou, Lord, shouldest mark iniquities, O Lord, who shall stand? But there is forgiveness with Thee, that Thou mayest be feared.

I wait for the Lord, my soul doth wait, and in His Word do I hope. My soul waiteth for the Lord more than they that watch for the morning; I say, more than they that watch for the morning.

Let Israel hope in the Lord; for with the Lord there is mercy, and with Him is plenteous redemption. And He shall redeem Israel from all his iniquities.

# The Evening Prayer

OUT of the depth of my troubled soul I cry to Thee, gracious Father, seeking refuge under the shadow of Thy wing, and healing from all my sin at the Cross of Jesus. I bring to Thee all the heartaches and sorrows, the burdens and cares, of my distressed life. Show to me and our household Thy mercy, and lift us out of all our troubles.

We are mindful of our many trespasses and sins. We know they have offended and grieved Thee. Nevertheless we come just as we are, unworthy and undeserving, believing Thy promises. Fulfill them upon us, and blot out all our transgressions with the precious blood of Thy Son, our Savior.

Wherever there are souls blackened by sin, aching hearts conscious of their faults, lives embittered because of the trials and troubles of the day, send Thy Gospel that such souls may find forgiveness, peace, hope, and salvation. This we ask of Thee because Jesus our Redeemer has died for all, that all may find forgiveness and peace. Amen.

## THE EVENING HYMN

Jesus, Lover of my soul,
    Let me to Thy bosom fly
While the nearer waters roll,
    While the tempest still is high.
Hide me, O my Savior, hide,
    Till the storm of life is past;
Safe into the haven guide.
    Oh, receive my soul at last!

Other refuge have I none;
    Hangs my helpless soul on Thee.
Leave, ah, leave me not alone,
    Still support and comfort me!

All my trust on Thee is stayed,
   All my help from Thee I bring;
Cover my defenseless head
   With the shadow of Thy wing.

Plenteous grace with Thee is found,
   Grace to cover all my sin.
Let the healing streams abound;
   Make and keep me pure within.
Thou of life the Fountain art,
   Freely let me take of Thee;
Spring Thou up within my heart,
   Rise to all eternity. Amen.

# Friday Morning

## I Corinthians 13

THOUGH I speak with the tongues of men and of angels and have not charity (or love), I am become as sounding brass or a tinkling cymbal. And though I have the gift of prophecy and understand all mysteries and all knowledge, and though I have all faith, so that I could remove mountains, and have not charity, I am nothing. And though I bestow all my goods to feed the poor, and though I give my body to be burned, and have not charity, it profiteth me nothing.

Charity suffereth long and is kind; charity envieth not; charity vaunteth not itself, is not puffed up, doth not behave itself unseemly, seeketh not her own, is not easily provoked, thinketh no evil; rejoiceth not in iniquity, but rejoiceth in the truth; beareth all things, believeth all things, hopeth all things, endureth all things.

Charity never faileth; but whether there be prophecies, they shall fail; whether there be tongues, they shall cease; whether there be knowledge, it shall vanish away. For we know in part, and we prophesy in part. But when that which is perfect is come, then that which is in part shall be done away.

When I was a child, I spake as a child, I understood as a child, I thought as a child:

but when I became a man, I put away child-
ish things. For now we see through a glass,
darkly; but then face to face; now I know in
part, but then shall I know even as also I
am known.

And now abideth faith, hope, charity,
these three; but the greatest of these is charity.

# The Morning Prayer

OUR hearts rejoice, eternal Keeper of our
souls, as we remember Thy boundless
love in Christ Jesus. Thou hast accepted us
into Thy family and made us heirs of the
eternal mansions. Grant us an abundance of
faith, love, and hope, that we may go on with
courage and confidence, winning victories
one day after another over sin and temptation, doubts and fears.

Grant that we may at no time be discouraged or disheartened, even as we look
through a glass, darkly, and the nights of

trouble seem long and endless. Lead us to the Cross to behold Thy love and grace, and then give us the assurance that Thou wilt not leave us nor fail us as we pass through the fiery trials of this present world.

Forgive us our murmurings. Give us strength to bear patiently the abuses heaped upon us, and keep us humble and pure, steadfast in faith, and diligent in Thy service. Through Jesus Christ, our Lord, who pleads for us in every hour of trial. Amen.

## THE MORNING HYMN

Take my life and let it be
Consecrated, Lord, to Thee;
Take my moments and my days,
Let them flow in ceaseless praise.

Take my hands and let them move
At the impulse of Thy love;
Take my feet and let them be
Swift and beautiful for Thee.

Take my voice and let me sing
Always, only, for my King;
Take my lips and let them be
Filled with messages from Thee.

Take my will and make it Thine,
It shall be no longer mine;
Take my heart, it is Thine own,
It shall be Thy royal throne.

Take my love, my Lord, I pour
At Thy feet its treasure-store;
Take myself, and I will be
Ever, only, all for Thee. Amen.

# Friday Evening
## Isaiah 43

BUT NOW, thus saith the Lord that created thee, O Jacob, and He that formed thee, O Israel, Fear not; for I have redeemed thee, I have called thee by thy name, thou art Mine. When thou passest through the waters, I will be with thee; and through the rivers, they shall not overflow thee; when thou walkest through the fire, thou shalt not be burned, neither shall the flame kindle upon thee. For I am the Lord, thy God, the Holy One of Israel, thy Savior.

But thou hast not called upon Me, O Jacob; but thou hast been weary of Me, O Israel. Thou hast not brought Me the small cattle of thy burnt offerings, neither hast thou honored Me with thy sacrifices. I have not caused thee to serve with an offering nor wearied thee with incense. Thou hast bought

Me no sweet cane with money, neither hast thou filled Me with the fat of thy sacrifices; but thou hast made Me to serve with thy sins, thou hast wearied Me with thine iniquities. I, even I, am He that blotted out thy transgressions for Mine own sake and will not remember thy sins.

# The Evening Prayer

THOU art acquainted with every step that we take throughout the day, O Lord, and hast written our name in the Book of Life, assuring to each one of us that we are precious in Thy sight. We confess that we have not deserved such protection and consideration, for we have often offended Thee with our disobedience and our neglecting to do Thy will. Other interests have made us forgetful of Thee. O Lord, remember not our sins, but for Jesus' sake remove them, and cover us with His righteousness, that we may be able to stand in Thy judgment unafraid and uncondemned.

Give to our household daily bread, and feed our souls with heavenly manna. Blot not our names out of Thy remembrance, but daily be with us to guide our footsteps and to uphold us in the hour of temptation. Then Thine shall be the praise until our journey's end in Christ Jesus. Amen.

## THE EVENING HYMN

Am I a soldier of the Cross,
  A follower of the Lamb.
And shall I fear to own His cause
  Or blush to speak His name?

Must I be carried to the skies
  On flowery beds of ease
While others fought to win the prize
  And sailed through bloody seas?

Are there no foes for me to face?
  Must I not stem the flood?
Is this vile world a friend to grace
  To help me on to God?

Sure I must fight if I would reign;
    Increase my courage, Lord!
I'll bear the toil, endure the pain,
    Supported by Thy Word.

Thy saints in all this glorious war
    Shall conquer though they die;
They see the triumph from afar
    With faith's discerning eye.

When that illustrious day shall rise
    And all Thine armies shine
In robes of victory through the skies,
    The glory shall be Thine.  Amen.

# Saturday Morning

## Revelation 7

AFTER this I beheld, and, lo, a great multitude, which no man could number, of all nations and kindreds and people and tongues, stood before the throne and before the Lamb, clothed with white robes and palms in

their hands; and cried with a loud voice, saying, Salvation to our God, which sitteth upon
the throne, and unto the Lamb. And all the
angels stood round about the throne and about
the elders and the four beasts, and fell before
the throne on their faces and worshiped God,
saying, Amen. Blessing, and glory, and
wisdom, and thanksgiving, and honor, and
power, and might be unto our God forever
and ever. Amen.

And one of the elders answered, saying
unto me, What are these which are arrayed
in white robes? And whence came they? And
I said unto him, Sir, thou knowest. And he
said to me, These are they which came out
of great tribulation, and have washed their
robes and made them white in the blood of
the Lamb. Therefore are they before the
throne of God, and serve Him day and night
in His temple; and He that sitteth on the
throne shall dwell among them. They shall
hunger no more, neither thirst any more;

neither shall the sun light on them nor any heat. For the Lamb which is in the midst of the throne shall feed them, and shall lead them unto living fountains of waters.

And God shall wipe away all tears from their eyes.

# The Morning Prayer

IN THIS morning hour, Lord Jesus, Lamb of God that takest away the sins of the world, we unite our hearts and voices in praise to Thee that we are numbered with Thy saints here on earth. We, too, have on robes washed white, and daily are clothed in the garment of Thy righteousness. We give to Thee blessing and glory, wisdom and thanksgiving, honor and power and might, day after day.

With expectancy we look forward to our eternal deliverance from the sorrows and sufferings and heartaches of this life, from the anxieties and trials of the day. To know that by Thy grace there is room even for us in the many mansions of heaven fills us with joy and peace.

We pray Thee, compassionate Savior, that none of this household and family miss the glory which is Thine from all eternity. Keep us faithful unto the end, that we may stand before Thy throne with a countless multitude to praise Thee, the Lamb that was slain, but now lives and reigns forever. Amen.

## THE MORNING HYMN

Ten thousand times ten thousand
    In sparkling raiment bright,
The armies of the ransomed saints
    Throng up the steeps of light.
'Tis finished, all is finished,
    Their fight with death and sin;
Fling open wide the golden gates
    And let the victors in.

What rush of alleluias
  Fills all the earth and sky!
What ringing of a thousand harps
  Proclaims the triumph nigh!
O day, for which creation
  And all its tribes were made!
O joy, for all its former woes
  A thousandfold repaid!

Oh, then what raptured greetings
  On Canaan's happy shore!
What knitting severed friendships up
  Where partings are no more!
Then eyes with joy shall sparkle
  That brimmed with tears of late;
Orphans no longer fatherless
  Nor widows desolate.

Bring near Thy great salvation,
  Thou Lamb for sinners slain;
Fill up the roll of Thine elect,
  Then take Thy power and reign.
Appear, Desire of Nations;
  Thine exiles long for home.
Show in the heavens Thy promised sign;
  Thou Prince and Savior, come! Amen.

# Saturday Evening

## Psalm 122

I WAS glad when they said unto me, Let us go into the house of the Lord. Our feet shall stand within thy gates, O Jerusalem. Jerusalem is builded as a city that is compact together, whither the tribes go up, the tribes of the Lord, unto the testimony of Israel to give thanks unto the name of the Lord. For there are set thrones of judgment, the thrones of the house of David.

Pray for the peace of Jerusalem. They shall prosper that love thee. Peace be within thy walls, and prosperity within thy palaces. For my brethren and companions' sakes I will now say, Peace be within thee. Because of the house of the Lord, our God, I will seek thy good.

# The Evening Prayer

AS we come to the close of another day and another week, Lord Jehovah, we thank Thee that Thou hast so graciously opened Thy hand to supply us with all the needs of this earthly life. Grant that we may acknowledge with grateful hearts and sacrificing hands Thy goodness as we come to Thy sanctuary tomorrow to hear Thy Word and receive Thy benediction. Prepare our hearts to receive the Word of Reconciliation with gladness, and cause us to bring forth fruits of Christian living a hundredfold. Forgive us all our sins, and abide with us with Thy protecting presence this coming night.

Bless the pastor, all pastors, as they prepare the message of peace. Let Thy Word reach many ears and hearts, and add many to Thy household. Grant us all that peace which can be received only through the atoning sacrifice of Jesus, Thy Son, our Lord, to whom, with Thee and the Holy Ghost, be praise and glory forever. Amen.

## THE EVENING HYMN

Lamp of our feet whereby we trace
  Our path when wont to stray;
Stream from the fount of heavenly grace,
  Brook by the traveler's way;

Bread of our souls whereon we feed,
  True manna from on high;
Our guide and chart wherein we read
  Of realms beyond the sky;

Pillar of fire, through watches dark,
  Or radiant cloud by day;
When waves would break our tossing bark,
  Our anchor and our stay:

Word of the ever-living God,
  Will of His glorious Son;
Without Thee, how could earth be trod
  Or heaven itself be won?

Lord, grant us all aright to learn
  The wisdom it imparts
And to its heavenly teaching turn
  With simple, childlike hearts.  Amen.

# Treasures of Hope

# THE THIRD WEEK

## Sunday Morning

# Romans 5

THEREFORE, being justified by faith, we have peace with God through our Lord Jesus Christ; by whom also we have access by faith into this grace wherein we stand, and rejoice in hope of the glory of God. And not only so, but we glory in tribulations also, knowing that tribulation worketh patience; and patience, experience; and experience, hope; and hope maketh not ashamed; because the love of God is shed abroad in our hearts by the Holy Ghost, which is given unto us. For when we were yet without strength, in due time Christ died for the ungodly. For scarcely for a righteous man will one die; yet peradventure for a good man some would even dare to die. But God commendeth His love toward us in that, while we were yet sinners, Christ died for us. Much more, then, being now justified by His blood, we shall be saved from wrath through Him.

For if, when we were enemies, we were reconciled to God by the death of His Son, much more, being reconciled, we shall be saved by His life. And not only so, but we also joy in God through our Lord Jesus Christ, by whom we have now received the atonement.

# The Morning Prayer

PEACE with Thee, O God—what blessed thought! To know that Thou art reconciled through Christ Jesus and that we are redeemed by Thy Son on Calvary even before we were born! This fills our hearts with wonderment and awe. Grant us the grace to appreciate daily Thy love in Christ, and grant that we by faith hold fast to this promise that the blood of Jesus cleanses us continually from all sins. Keep us standing in Thy grace, fill our hearts with the joy of forgiveness, and enrich our lives with the glorious hope and certainty of our salvation.

Sinners, yet saints by grace, we come to Thee with all our vexing problems and anxious thoughts. We place them at Thy feet as our gracious Father in Christ.

As Thy Word of Reconciliation sounds forth today from all Christian pulpits, grant that thousands and ten thousands look up in faith to the Savior from sin and be justified in Thy presence and find peace and rest for their souls, even as we have found it in the uplifted Christ, our eternal Mediator. Amen.

## THE MORNING HYMN

Blessed Jesus, at Thy word
  We are gathered all to hear Thee;
Let our hearts and souls be stirred
  Now to seek and love and fear Thee,
By Thy teachings, sweet and holy,
Drawn from earth to love Thee solely.

All our knowledge, sense, and sight
  Lie in deepest darkness shrouded
Till Thy Spirit breaks our night
  With the beams of truth unclouded.
Thou alone to God canst win us;
Thou must work all good within us.

Glorious Lord, Thyself impart,
  Light of Light, from God proceeding;
Open Thou our ears and heart,
  Help us by Thy Spirit's pleading;
Hear the cry Thy people raises,
Hear and bless our prayers and praises.

Father, Son, and Holy Ghost,
  Praise to Thee and adoration!
Grant that we Thy Word may trust
  And obtain true consolation
While we here below must wander,
Till we sing Thy praises yonder. Amen.

# Sunday Evening

# John 3

THERE was a man of the Pharisees, named Nicodemus, a ruler of the Jews. The same came to Jesus by night and said unto Him, Rabbi, we know that Thou art a teacher come from God; for no man can do these miracles that Thou doest, except God be with him. Jesus answered and said unto him, Verily, verily, I say unto thee, Except a man be born again, he cannot see the kingdom of God. Nicodemus saith unto Him, How can a man be born when he is old? Can he enter the second time into his mother's womb and be born? Jesus answered, Verily, verily, I say unto thee, Except a man be born of water and of the Spirit, he cannot enter into the kingdom of God. That which is born of the flesh is flesh; and that which is born of the Spirit is spirit.

Marvel not that I said unto thee, Ye must be born again. The wind bloweth where it listeth, and thou hearest the sound thereof, but canst not tell whence it cometh and whither it goeth: so is every one that is born of the Spirit. Nicodemus answered and said unto Him, How can these things be? Jesus answered and said unto him, Art thou a master of Israel and knowest not these things? Verily, verily, I say unto thee, We speak that We do know, and testify that We have seen; and ye receive not Our witness. If I have told you earthly things and ye believe not, how shall ye believe if I tell you of heavenly things? And no man hath ascended up to heaven but He that came down from heaven, even the Son of Man, which is in heaven.

And as Moses lifted up the serpent in the wilderness, even so must the Son of Man be lifted up, that whosoever believeth in Him should not perish, but have eternal life. For

God so loved the world that He gave His only-begotten Son, that whosoever believeth in Him should not perish, but have everlasting life.

For God sent not His Son into the world to condemn the world, but that the world through Him might be saved. He that believeth on Him is not condemned; but he that believeth not is condemned already because he hath not believed in the name of the only-begotten Son of God.

And this is the condemnation, that light is come into the world and men loved darkness rather than light, because their deeds were evil. For everyone that doeth evil hateth the light, neither cometh to the light, lest his deeds should be reproved. But he that doeth truth cometh to the light, that his deeds may be made manifest, that they are wrought in God.

# The Evening Prayer

LORD JESUS, crucified for our transgressions and forsaken on the Cross because of our sins, look with compassion on us, and let no unforgiven sin remain with us this night. Thy Word has nourished our souls and strengthened our faith. Joy filled our hearts and praise our lips as we heard today again the Gospel of peace, which gives us the glorious assurance that whosoever believeth in Thee shall not perish, but have everlasting life.

We thank Thee, Savior of the lost, that Thou hast preserved Thy Christian Church in our midst to this very day. Fill our hearts with the eager desire and with fervent zeal to build Thy Zion and spread Thy kingdom.

Grant courage and strength to all ministers of the Gospel to proclaim Thy Word without fear or favor. Bless them and keep them faithful to Thy revelations. Bless the missionaries in all parts of the world, and let them see the fruits of their labors. Give them the joy of seeing many souls added to Thy Church.

And to us grant faithfulness to the end, that Thy Word may dwell in our homes and Thy peace in our hearts until time ends and eternity begins. Amen.

## THE EVENING HYMN

Christ, Thou art the sure Foundation,
  Thou the Head and Cornerstone,
Chosen of the Lord and precious,
  Binding all the Church in one;
Thou Thy Zion's Help forever
  And her Confidence alone.

To this temple, where we call Thee,
  Come, O Lord of hosts, today;
With Thy wonted loving-kindness
  Hear Thy servants as they pray,
And Thy fullest benediction
  Shed within these walls alway.

Here vouchsafe to all Thy servants
  What they ask of Thee to gain,
What they gain from Thee forever
  With the blessed to retain,
And hereafter in Thy glory
  Evermore with Thee to reign.

Praise and honor to the Father,
  Praise and honor to the Son,
Praise and honor to the Spirit,
  Ever Three and ever One,
One in might and one in glory,
  While unending ages run.  Amen.

# Monday Morning

## Psalm 119

BLESSED are the undefiled in the way,
who walk in the Law of the Lord. Blessed
are they that keep His testimonies and that
seek Him with the whole heart. I will praise
Thee with uprightness of heart when I shall
have learned Thy righteous judgments. I will
keep Thy statutes. Oh, forsake me not utterly!

Thy Word have I hid in mine heart that
I might not sin against Thee. Blessed art
Thou, O Lord; teach me Thy statutes. Teach
me, O Lord, the way of Thy statutes, and I
shall keep it unto the end. Give me understanding, and I shall keep Thy Law; yea, I
shall observe it with my whole heart.

Oh, how love I Thy Law! It is my meditation all the day. I have refrained my feet
from every evil way that I might keep Thy

Word. I have not departed from Thy judgments, for Thou has taught me. How sweet are Thy words unto my taste! yea, sweeter than honey to my mouth. Through Thy precepts I get understanding; therefore I hate every false way. Thy Word is a lamp unto my feet and a light unto my path.

Thy testimonies are wonderful; therefore doth my soul keep them. The entrance of Thy words giveth light; it giveth understanding unto the simple. Look Thou upon me and be merciful unto me, as Thou usest to do unto those that love Thy name.

Order my steps in Thy Word, and let not any iniquity have dominion over Me. Make Thy face to shine upon Thy servant, and teach me Thy statutes.

Let my soul live, and it shall praise Thee; and let Thy judgments help me.

# The Morning Prayer

IN Thy name, Lord Jesus, eternal God, we begin this day and our week of work to obtain our daily bread. Bless Thou the labors of our hands and minds, and grant us faithfulness in performing our duties and meeting our obligations. Most of all we beseech Thee to guard us from sin and evil. Help us to walk the Christian way, doing Thy will and carrying out Thy commission to bear witness of Thee by word and conduct. Forgive us graciously and guide and direct our lives through Thy Word.

Abide in our homes with Thy peace, and grace our hearts with contentment and a forgiving spirit. Let the sunshine of Thy love spread itself over all our day, and let Thy righteousness cover us. Cause the peoples of the earth to praise Thee from one end of the world to the other to the glory of Thine own immortal name. Amen.

## THE MORNING HYMN

Oh, blest the house, whate'er befall,
Where Jesus Christ is all in all!
Yea, if He were not dwelling there,
How poor and dark and void it were!

Oh, blest that house where faith ye find
And all within have set their mind
To trust their God and serve Him still
And do in all His holy will!

Oh, blest the parents who give heed
Unto their children's foremost need
And weary not of care or cost!
May none to them and heaven be lost!

Blest such a house, it prospers well;
In peace and joy the parents dwell,
And in their children's lot is shown
How richly God can bless His own.

Then here will I and mine today
A solemn covenant make and say:
Though all the world forsake Thy Word,
I and my house will serve the Lord.
                                    Amen.

# 𝔐onday 𝔈bening

## Psalm 19

THE heavens declare the glory of God, and the firmament showeth His handiwork. Day unto day uttereth speech, and night unto night showeth knowledge. There is no speech nor language where their voice is not heard. Their line is gone out through all the earth, and their words to the end of the world. In them hath He set a tabernacle for the sun, which is as a bridegroom coming out of his chamber, and rejoiceth as a strong man to run a race. His going forth is from the end of the heaven, and his circuit unto the ends of it; and there is nothing hid from the heat thereof.

The Law of the Lord is perfect, converting the soul; the testimony of the Lord is sure, making wise the simple. The statutes of the

Lord are right, rejoicing the heart; the commandment of the Lord is pure, enlightening the eyes. The fear of the Lord is clean, enduring for ever, the judgments of the Lord are true and righteous altogether. More to be desired are they than gold, yea, than much fine gold; sweeter also than honey and the honeycomb. Moreover, by them is Thy servant warned, and in keeping of them there is great reward.

Who can understand his errors? Cleanse Thou me from secret faults. Keep back Thy servant also from presumptuous sins; let them not have dominion over me; then shall I be upright, and I shall be innocent from the great transgression. Let the words of my mouth and the meditation of my heart be acceptable in Thy sight, O Lord, My Strength and My Redeemer.

# The Evening Prayer

ACCEPT, righteous yet gracious God, the praise of our lips and the adoration of our hearts. With all Thy people we acknowledge Thee as the only God and Jesus Christ, Thy Son, as the only Savior of mankind. Thou hast been good to us, breaking daily the bread necessary for our needs. Thou hast been merciful, forgiving us every transgression of Thy Law and keeping us in Thy grace.

Remove from our hearts all worrisome thoughts, and grant that at no time we doubt Thy Word and promises. Open Thou our understanding that we may grow in knowledge of Thee and walk in the paths of Thy commandments.

With the heavens we declare Thy glory, and with the angels we sing Thy praise, and with the saints and believers we thank Thee who hast sent Thy Son, Jesus Christ, into the world to make us Thine own through His precious sacrifice.

Preserve us in faith and make us rich in service to Thee and our fellow men for Jesus' sake. Amen.

## THE EVENING HYMN

Now rest beneath night's shadow
The woodland, field, and meadow,
　The world in slumber lies;
But thou, my heart, awake thee,
To prayer and song betake thee;
　Let praise to thy Creator rise.

The radiant sun hath vanished,
His golden rays are banished
　By night, the foe of day;
But Christ, the Sun of gladness,
Dispelling all my sadness,
　Within my heart holds constant sway.

Lord Jesus, who dost love me,
Oh, spread Thy wings above me
　And shield me from alarm!
Though evil would assail me,
Thy mercy will not fail me:
　I rest in Thy protecting arm. Amen.

# Tuesday Morning

## Luke 12

AND He said unto His disciples, Therefore I say unto you, Take no thought for your life, what ye shall eat; neither for the body, what ye shall put on. The life is more than meat, and the body is more than raiment. Consider the ravens: for they neither sow nor reap, which neither have storehouses nor barn, and God feedeth them: how much more are ye better than the fowls! And which of you with taking thought can add to his stature one cubit? If ye, then, be not able to do that thing which is least, why take ye thought for the rest?

Consider the lilies, how they grow; they toil not, they spin not; and yet I say unto you that Solomon in all his glory was not arrayed like one of these. If, then, God so clothe the grass, which is today in the field and tomorrow is cast into the oven, how much more will He clothe you, O ye of little faith! And seek not ye what ye shall eat or what ye shall drink, neither be ye of doubtful mind. For all these things do the nations of the world seek after, and your Father knoweth that ye have need of these things. But rather seek ye the kingdom of God, and all these things shall be added unto you. Fear not, little flock; for it is your Father's good pleasure to give you the Kingdom.

Sell that ye have and give alms; provide yourselves bags which wax not old, a treasure in the heavens that faileth not, where no thief approacheth neither moth corrupteth. For where your treasure is, there will your heart be also. Let your loins be girded about and your lights burning.

And ye yourselves like unto men that wait for their lord when he will return from the wedding, that, when he cometh and

knocketh, they may open unto him imme-
diately. Blessed are those servants whom the
lord, when he cometh, shall find watching;
verily I say unto you that he shall gird himself and make them to sit down to meat, and
will come forth and serve them.

# The Morning Prayer

TAKE me by the hand, heavenly Father in
Christ Jesus, and lead me step by step
along life's rough and troublous way. Without Thee my footsteps falter; without Thee I
am uncertain, blinded, and confused.

O Lord, hide all of us in the folds of Thy
grace as we pass through the shadows and
anxieties of the day. Keep us from stumbling,
falling, and injuring ourselves. We need not
be afraid nor fretful as long as Thou art at
our side. Therefore we seek refuge with Thee
at the beginning of this day.

Remember not our sins and forgive us all our worryings. Grant that we set our face continually to the Cross and believe that through Christ Crucified we are Thy children, forgiven and saved.

Strengthen our faith. Show us Thy loving-kindness through the promises of Thy Word. Bless each and every soul which trusts in Thee. Watch especially over the sick, the lonely, the aged, and the discouraged. As Thou hast promised, so be it, for Jesus' sake. Amen.

## THE MORNING HYMN

With the Lord begin thy task,
 Jesus will direct it;
For His aid and counsel ask,
 Jesus will perfect it.
Every morn with Jesus rise,
 And when day is ended,
In His name then close thine eyes;
 Be to Him commended.

Let each day begin with prayer,
  Praise, and adoration;
On the Lord cast every care,
  He is thy salvation.
Morning, evening, and at night
  Jesus will be near thee,
Save thee from the Tempter's might,
  With His presence cheer thee.

If thy task be thus begun
  With the Savior's blessing,
Safely then thy course will run,
  Naught thy soul distressing.
Good will follow everywhere
  While thou here must wander;
Thou at last the joy wilt share
  In the mansions yonder.

Thus, Lord Jesus, every task
  Be to Thee commended;
May Thy will be done, I ask,
  Until life is ended.
Jesus, in Thy name begun
  Be the day's endeavor;
Grant that it may well be done
  To Thy praise forever. Amen.

# Tuesday Evening

# John 14

LET not your heart be troubled; ye believe in God, believe also in Me. In My Father's house are many mansions; if it were not so, I would have told you. I go to prepare a place for you. And if I go and prepare a place for you, I will come again and receive you unto Myself, that where I am, there ye may be also. And whither I go ye know, and the way ye know. Thomas saith unto Him, Lord, we know not whither Thou goest; and how can we know the way? Jesus saith unto him, I am the Way, the Truth, and the Life; no man cometh unto the Father but by Me.

Verily, verily, I say unto you, He that believeth on Me, the works that I do shall he do also; and greater works than these shall he do, because I go unto My Father. And whatsoever ye shall ask in My name, that will I do, that the Father may be glorified in the Son. If ye shall ask anything in My name, I will do it.

If ye love Me, keep My commandments. And I will pray the Father, and He shall give you another Comforter that He may abide with you forever, even the Spirit of Truth, whom the world cannot receive, because it seeth Him not, neither knoweth Him. But ye know Him, for He dwelleth with you and shall be in you. I will not leave you comfortless; I will come to you.

If a man love Me, he will keep My Words; and My Father will love him, and We will come unto him, and make Our abode with him. He that loveth Me not keepeth not My sayings; and the Word which ye hear is not Mine, but the Father's which sent Me. These things have I spoken unto you, being yet present with you. But the Comforter, which is the Holy Ghost, whom the Father will send in My name, He shall teach you all things and bring all things to your remembrance, whatsoever I have said unto you. Peace I leave with you, My peace I give unto you; not as the world giveth, give I unto you. Let not your heart be troubled, neither let it be afraid.

# The Evening Prayer

LORD JESUS, Strength of the weary and Friend of the troubled, we come to Thee with all the burdens of the day, asking Thee to give us contented hearts and relaxed minds. Take from our hearts and minds all sinful thoughts, all rebellious thoughts, and all anxious thoughts. Let us find peace in Thee.

As we close our eyes in sleep, let this thought go with us that we are forgiven and protected of Thee. Grant that this joy of forgiveness and the hope of salvation be ours all through the years which lie ahead of us.

Bless this household from day to day, and keep us steadfast in faith and standing in Thy grace. Grant that we believe with confident heart that underneath are Thine everlasting arms to uphold us amid all the trials of this present world.

Give to us peaceful days and restful nights, unworried minds and untroubled hearts. Keep us close to Thee, who hast redeemed us with Thine own precious blood. Amen.

## THE EVENING HYMN

Be still, my soul; the Lord is on thy side;
  Bear patiently the cross of grief and pain;
Leave to thy God to order and provide;
  In every change He faithful will remain.
Be still, my soul; thy best, thy heavenly
    Friend
Through thorny ways leads to a joyful end.

Be still, my soul, though dearest friends
    depart
  And all is darkened in the vale of tears;
Then shalt thou better know His love, His
    heart,
  Who comes to soothe thy sorrows and
    thy fears.
Be still, my soul; thy Jesus can repay
From His own fullness all He takes away.

Be still, my soul; the hour is hastening on
  When we shall be forever with the Lord,
When disappointment, grief, and fear are
    gone,
  Sorrow forgot, love's purest joy restored.
Be still, my soul; when change and tears
    are past,
All safe and blessed we shall meet at last.
                          Amen.

# Wednesday Morning

## Psalm 145

I WILL extol Thee, my God, O King, and I will bless Thy name forever and ever. Every day will I bless Thee, and I will praise Thy name forever and ever. Great is the Lord and greatly to be praised, and His greatness is unsearchable. One generation shall praise Thy works to another and shall declare Thy mighty acts. I will speak of the glorious honor of Thy majesty and of Thy wondrous works. And men shall speak of the might of Thy terrible acts, and I will declare Thy greatness. They shall abundantly utter the memory of Thy great goodness and shall sing of Thy righteousness.

The Lord is gracious and full of compassion, slow to anger, and of great mercy. The Lord is good to all, and His tender mercies are over all His works. All Thy works shall praise Thee, O Lord, and Thy saints shall bless Thee. They shall speak of the glory of Thy kingdom and talk of Thy power, to make known to the sons of men His mighty acts and the glorious majesty of His kingdom. Thy kingdom is an everlasting kingdom, and Thy dominion endureth throughout all generations.

The Lord upholdeth all that fall and raiseth up all those that be bowed down. The eyes of all wait upon Thee, and Thou givest them their meat in due season. Thou openest Thine hand and satisfiest the desire of every living thing.

The Lord is righteous in all His ways and holy in all His works. The Lord is nigh unto all them that call upon Him, to all that call upon Him in truth. He will fulfill the desire of them that fear Him; He also will hear their cry and will save them. The Lord preserveth all them that love Him, but all the wicked will He destroy. My mouth shall speak the praise of the Lord; and let all flesh bless His holy name forever and ever.

# The Morning Prayer

LORD GOD, who never failest to supply us with the needs of this present life and hast given us Thy Word in abundance to nourish our souls, accept our thanks and praise in this early hour of the morning. Be with us also throughout the day.

Thou art a God of compassion and grace, forgiving sin and protecting us from the wiles of Satan. This knowledge and truth sends us on our way rejoicing, confident of Thy guidance and certain of Thy protection.

Give us the strength needed to perform those duties which we are called upon to do, and grant that we may do them with cheerfulness of heart. May we never fail to glorify Thy name nor forget to speak of Thy mercies.

Bless this household and each one of us as we go to and fro in our calling. Preserve to us Thy Word and Sacrament, and grant us grace to live normal and peaceable lives, protected from danger and defended from temptations.

Accept our praise and thanksgiving, arising from our believing hearts, in Christ Jesus, our Lord. Amen.

## THE MORNING HYMN

Oh, that I had a thousand voices
　To praise my God with thousand tongues!
My heart, which in the Lord rejoices,
　Would then proclaim in grateful songs
To all, wherever I might be,
What great things God hath done for me.

Dear Father, endless praise I render
　For soul and body, strangely joined;
I praise Thee, Guardian kind and tender,
　For all the noble joys I find
So richly spread on every side
And freely for my use supplied.

I praise Thee, Savior, whose compassion
  Did bring Thee down to ransom me;
Thy pitying heart sought my salvation
  Though keenest woes were heaped on Thee,
Brought me from bondage full release,
Made me Thine own, and gave me peace.

Glory and praise, still onward reaching,
  Be Thine, O Spirit of all grace,
Whose holy power and faithful teaching
  Give me among Thy saints a place.
Whate'er of good by me is done
Is wrought by grace divine alone.  Amen.

# Wednesday Evening

## Isaiah 54

SING, O barren, thou that didst not bear;
break forth into singing and cry aloud,
thou that didst not travail with child; for more
are the children of the desolate than the children of the married wife, saith the Lord.
Enlarge the place of thy tent, and let them
stretch forth the curtains of thine habitations;

spare not, lengthen thy cords, and strengthen thy stakes; for thou shalt break forth on the right hand and on the left, and thy seed shall inherit the Gentiles and make the desolate cities to be inhabited.

Fear not, for thou shalt not be ashamed; neither be thou confounded, for thou shalt not be put to shame; for thou shalt forget the shame of thy youth, and shalt not remember the reproach of thy widowhood any more. For thy Maker is thine Husband; the Lord of hosts is His name; and thy Redeemer, the Holy One of Israel. The God of the whole earth shall He be called. For the Lord hath called thee as a woman forsaken and grieved in spirit, and a wife of youth when thou wast refused, saith thy God.

For a small moment have I forsaken thee, but with great mercies will I gather thee. In a little wrath I hid My face from thee for a moment, but with everlasting kindness will I have mercy on thee, saith the

Lord, thy Redeemer. For this is as the waters of Noah unto Me; for as I have sworn that the waters of Noah should no more go over the earth, so have I sworn that I would not be wroth with thee nor rebuke thee.

For the mountains shall depart and the hills be removed, but My kindness shall not depart from thee, neither shall the covenant of My peace be removed, saith the Lord that hath mercy on thee.

# The Evening Prayer

THY covenant of peace has truly filled our hearts with joy, faithful Father in Christ Jesus. We would not dare to approach Thy throne if it were not for the redemption of the Cross, for we have displeased Thee with our neglects and offended Thee with our transgressions. But we come, unworthy though we be, pleading for mercy in Christ, whose precious blood cleanses from all sin. Turn not from us, O Lord, but embrace us with Thy love, and draw us closer to Thy fatherly heart.

Bring all Thy erring children back to Thee, and show to the straying the folly of living in unbelief and sin. Forsake none who call on Thee in the hour of temptation; let not Satan nor the world seduce and mislead us into believing that filled barns can satisfy the needs of our souls. Make us more determined to serve Thee, and keep us faithful to Thee and Thy Son Jesus Christ, who has redeemed us that we might be Thine forever. Amen.

## THE EVENING HYMN

Sun of my soul, Thou Savior dear,
It is not night if Thou be near.
Oh, may no earthborn cloud arise
To hide Thee from Thy servant's eyes!

When the soft dews of kindly sleep
My wearied eyelids gently steep,
Be my last thought how sweet to rest
Forever on my Savior's breast.

Abide with me from morn till eve,
For without Thee I cannot live;
Abide with me when night is nigh,
For without Thee I dare not die.

If some poor wandering child of Thine
Has spurned today the voice divine,
Now, Lord, the gracious work begin;
Let him no more lie down in sin.

Watch by the sick; enrich the poor
With blessings from Thy boundless store;
Be every mourner's sleep tonight,
Like infant's slumbers, pure and light.

Come near and bless us when we wake,
Ere through the world our way we take,
Till in the ocean of Thy love
We lose ourselves in heaven above. Amen.

# Thursday Morning

## Psalm 33

REJOICE in the Lord, O ye righteous; for praise is comely for the upright. Praise the Lord with harp; sing unto Him with the psaltery and an instrument of ten strings. Sing unto Him a new song; play skillfully with a loud noise. For the Word of the Lord is right, and all His works are done in truth. He loveth righteousness and judgment; the earth is full of the goodness of the Lord.

By the word of the Lord were the heavens made, and all the host of them by the breath of His mouth. He gathereth the waters of the sea together as an heap; He layeth up the depth in storehouses. Let all the earth fear the Lord; let all the inhabitants of the world stand in awe of Him. For He spake, and it was done; He commanded, and it stood fast. The Lord bringeth the counsel of the heathen to nought; He maketh the devices of the people of none effect. The counsel of the Lord standeth forever, the thoughts of His heart to all generations.

Blessed is the nation whose God is the Lord; and the people whom He hath chosen for His own inheritance. The Lord looketh from heaven; He beholdeth all the sons of men. From the place of His habitation He looketh upon all the inhabitants of the earth. He fashioneth their hearts alike; He considereth all their works. There is no king saved by the multitude of an host; a mighty man is not delivered by much strength. An horse is a vain thing for safety; neither shall he deliver any by his great strength.

Behold, the eye of the Lord is upon them that fear Him, upon them that hope in His mercy, to deliver their soul from death, and to keep them alive in famine. Our soul waiteth for the Lord; He is our Help and our Shield. For our heart shall rejoice in Him,

because we have trusted in His holy name.
Let Thy mercy, O Lord, be upon us, according as we hope in Thee.

# The Morning Prayer

BLESSED LORD, Thine is the kingdom from generation to generation; Thine the power to supply all the needs of body and soul; and therefore to Thee we give all the glory, praising Thee and making known to all that Thou art gracious and merciful. The earth is full of Thy goodness. Only our sins and the iniquity of the world have marred the beauty of life and robbed us of peace of mind. Forgive us, Lord, and keep us from stumbling and straying.

Through this day let Thy Word be a light to our path and Thy truth keep us from the ways of sin.

Bless this family and enrich our lives through the growing knowledge of Thy Word.

Strengthen our faith, and grant us nobility
of character, being rich in service to Thee
and our fellow men.

May we as a nation exalt uprightness;
let justice prevail in the courts. Grant that
we all may lead normal lives, defended from
the ravages of war and the deceitfulness of
sin. Let Thy mercy and goodness keep us in
Thy grace and in the kingdom of Jesus Christ,
our Lord. Amen.

## THE MORNING HYMN

How precious is the Book Divine,
  By inspiration given!
Bright as a lamp its doctrines shine
  To guide our souls to heaven.

Its light, descending from above
  Our gloomy world to cheer,
Displays a Savior's boundless love,
  And brings His glories near.

It shows to man his wandering ways
  And where his feet have trod,
And brings to view the matchless grace
  Of a forgiving God.

It sweetly cheers our drooping hearts
  In this dark vale of tears;
Life, light, and joy it still imparts
  And quells our rising fears.

This lamp through all the tedious night
  Of life shall guide our way
Till we behold the clearer light
  Of an eternal day. Amen.

# Thursday Evening

## Psalm 4

HEAR me when I call, O God of my righteousness. Thou hast enlarged me when I was in distress. Have mercy upon me and hear my prayer.

O ye sons of men, how long will ye turn My glory into shame? How long will ye love vanity and seek after leasing? Selah.

But know that the Lord hath set apart him that is godly for Himself; the Lord will hear when I call unto Him. Stand in awe,

and sin not; commune with your own heart
upon your bed, and be still. Selah. Offer the
sacrifices of righteousness, and put your trust
in the Lord. There be many that say, Who
will show us any good?

Lord, lift Thou up the light of Thy countenance upon us. Thou hast put gladness in
my heart, more than in the time that their
corn and their wine increased. I will both
lay me down in peace and sleep; for Thou,
Lord, only makest me dwell in safety.

# The Evening Prayer

TO US, Thy children, heavenly Father,
Thou hast promised sleep and rest if we
place ourselves into Thy hands. Because
Thou dost not slumber nor sleep, we can
rest for the night untroubled and without fear.

Watch over all Thy children, especially
those who are in pain or sorrowing. Draw

nigh to them in the long hours of the night and speak peace to their souls. Place them into Thine everlasting arms, that despondency or despair may not crush them.

Forgive us our distrustful thoughts and worries. Teach us to know that we need not fear anything in life or death as long as we hide in the sacred wounds of Thy Son Jesus Christ, who has purchased us with His own blood and made us kings and priests to live with Him forever. May the hope of this fullness of joy make us patient amid the disappointments, heartaches, and sufferings of this present life. Keep us near the Cross of Jesus all along the journey of life for His sake. Amen.

## THE EVENING HYMN

O God, our Help in ages past,
　Our Hope for years to come,
Our Shelter from the stormy blast,
　And our eternal Home!

Under the shadow of Thy throne
　Thy saints have dwelt secure;
Sufficient is Thine arm alone,
　And our defense is sure.

Before the hills in order stood
　Or earth received her frame,
From everlasting Thou art God,
　To endless years the same.

A thousand ages in Thy sight
　Are like an evening gone,
Short as the watch that ends the night
　Before the rising sun.

O God, our Help in ages past,
　Our Hope for years to come,
Be Thou our Guard while troubles last
　And our eternal Home. Amen.

# Friday Morning

## Psalm 91

HE THAT dwelleth in the secret place of the Most High shall abide under the shadow of the Almighty. I will say of the Lord, He is my Refuge and my Fortress, my God; in Him will I trust. Surely He shall deliver thee from the snare of the fowler and from the noisome pestilence. He shall cover thee with His feathers, and under His wings shalt thou trust; His truth shall be thy shield and buckler.

Thou shalt not be afraid for the terror by night, nor for the arrow that flieth by day, nor for the pestilence that walketh in darkness, nor for the destruction that wasteth at noonday. A thousand shall fall at thy side and ten thousand at thy right hand, but it shall not come nigh thee. Only with thine eyes shalt thou behold and see the reward of the wicked. Because thou hast made the Lord, which is my Refuge, even the Most High, thy Habitation; there shall no evil befall thee, neither shall any plague come nigh thy dwelling.

For He shall give His angels charge over thee to keep thee in all thy ways. They shall bear thee up in their hands lest thou dash thy foot against a stone. Thou shalt tread upon the lion and adder; the young lion and the dragon shalt thou trample under feet.

Because He hath set his love upon Me, therefore will I deliver him; I will set him on high, because he hath known My name. He shall call upon Me, and I will answer him; I will be with him in trouble; I will deliver him and honor him. With long life will I satisfy him and show him My salvation.

# The Morning Prayer

ALMIGHTY GOD, eternal Lord, Thou alone art able to protect us every hour of this day. We beseech Thee, guard and preserve us and all Thy children from harm and danger, temptation, and sin. Death and destruction are surrounding us on all sides; but Thou, O Lord, art our sure Defense and our immediate Help in every trouble. Send Thy holy angels to watch over us and especially over the little children, lest they fall and stumble and suffer injury.

As Thou givest life and health to us day after day, show us the greater treasures, and let us find salvation, contentment, peace, and joy in the one thing needful

In Thy name we begin the tasks and duties at hand and ask Thee to bless us as we go out and as we come into this home, where we ask Thee to abide with Thy Son Jesus Christ. Amen.

## THE MORNING HYMN

Guide me, O Thou great Jehovah,
  Pilgrim through this barren land.
I am weak, but Thou art mighty;
  Hold me with Thy powerful hand.
    Bread of heaven,
Feed me till I want no more.

Open now the crystal fountain
  Whence the healing stream doth flow;
Let the fiery, cloudy pillar
  Lead me all my journey through.
    Strong Deliverer,
Be Thou still my Strength and Shield.

When I tread the verge of Jordan,
  Bid my anxious fears subside;
Death of death and hell's Destruction,
  Land me safe on Canaan's side.
    Songs of praises
I will ever give to Thee. Amen.

# Friday Evening
## Colossians 3

PUT on therefore, as the elect of God, holy and beloved, bowels of mercies, kindness, humbleness of mind, meekness, long-suffering, forbearing one another, and forgiving one another if any man have a quarrel against any; even as Christ forgave you, so also do ye. And above all these things put on charity, which is the bond of perfectness.

And let the peace of God rule in your hearts, to the which also ye are called in one body; and be ye thankful.

Let the Word of Christ dwell in you richly in all wisdom; teaching and admonishing one another in psalms and hymns and spiritual songs, singing with grace in your hearts to the Lord.

And whatsoever ye do in word or deed, do all in the name of the Lord Jesus, giving thanks to God and the Father by Him.

# The Evening Prayer

BECAUSE Thou hast been our Stay and Strength, almighty God, we have come to the close of the day unharmed and children of Thy grace. As the day closes, enclose us with Thy protecting love, that we may sleep in peace as forgiven children of Thine. Remove from our hearts all bitterness and resentment against our fellow men. In Christ Thou hast so graciously forgiven us; make us forgiving, and grant that we do not close this day unreconciled. We beseech Thee to take full possession of us and to rule our hearts with Thy grace.

Bless this home and all that dwell in it, the Church of Thy Son Jesus Christ, this nation which we call our own. Grant that Thy Gospel may reach the ends of the earth and that more and more people of our country acknowledge Thee as their God, and Thy Son Jesus Christ as their Savior from sin.

Amen.

## THE EVENING HYMN

Savior, breathe an evening blessing
    Ere repose our spirits seal;
Sin and want we come confessing;
    Thou canst save, and Thou canst heal.

Though destruction walk around us,
    Though the arrows past us fly,
Angel guards from Thee surround us;
    We are safe if Thou art nigh.

Though the night be dark and dreary,
    Darkness cannot hide from Thee;
Thou art He who, never weary,
    Watchest where Thy people be.

Should swift death this night o'ertake us
    And our couch become our tomb,
May the morn in heaven awake us,
    Clad in light and deathless bloom.
                Amen.

# Saturday Morning

## Psalm 143

HEAR my prayer, O Lord, give ear to my supplications; in Thy faithfulness answer me, and in Thy righteousness. And enter not into judgment with Thy servant, for in Thy sight shall no man living be justified. For the enemy hath persecuted my soul; he hath smitten my life down to the ground; he hath made me to dwell in darkness, as those that have been long dead. Therefore is my spirit overwhelmed within me; my heart within me is desolate.

I remember the days of old; I meditate on all Thy works; I muse on the work of Thy hands. I stretch forth my hands unto Thee; my soul thirsteth after Thee as a thirsty land. Selah. Hear me speedily, O Lord; my spirit faileth; hide not Thy face from me lest

I be like unto them that go down into the pit. Cause me to hear Thy loving-kindness in the morning, for in Thee do I trust. Cause me to know the way wherein I should walk, for I lift up my soul unto Thee. Deliver me, O Lord, from mine enemies; I flee unto Thee to hide me.

Teach me to do Thy will, for Thou art my God. Thy spirit is good; lead me into the land of uprightness. Quicken me, O Lord, for Thy name's sake; for Thy righteousness' sake bring my soul out of trouble. And of Thy mercy cut off mine enemies, and destroy all them that afflict my soul; for I am Thy servant.

# The Morning Prayer

O GOD, Thou art *my* God. In this morning hour we seek Thee, as the Keeper of our body and the Lover of our soul in Christ Jesus. Without Thee we have no strength to resist Satan and sin; without Thy divine benediction the day would be trying and discouraging. In Thy faithfulness preserve us, and in Thy love be with us.

We confess that we are not deserving of this consideration, and solely plead mercy and grace as we come to Thee. Show us Thy way, and teach us to do Thy will, and lead us on the narrow way that brings us at last to glory. Stretch forth Thy hand, and protect us this day from all harm, and prepare our hearts to receive Thy Word with gladness. Then Thine shall be the praise of our thankful hearts in Christ Jesus, the Savior of all mankind. Amen.

# THE MORNING HYMN

Praise, oh, praise, our God and King,
Hymns of adoration sing;
For His mercies still endure,
Ever faithful, ever sure.

Praise Him that He made the sun
Day by day his course to run;
For His mercies still endure,
Ever faithful, ever sure.

Praise Him that He gave the rain
To mature the swelling grain;
For His mercies still endure,
Ever faithful, ever sure.

Praise Him for our harvest store,
He hath filled the garner floor;
For His mercies still endure,
Ever faithful, ever sure.

And for richer food than this,
Pledge of everlasting bliss;
For His mercies still endure,
Ever faithful, ever sure.

Glory to our bounteous King,
Glory let creation sing;
Glory to the Father, Son,
And the Spirit, Three in One! Amen.

# Saturday Evening

# John 10

THEN said Jesus unto them again, Verily, verily, I say unto you, I am the Door of the sheep. All that ever came before Me are thieves and robbers; but the sheep did not hear them. I am the Door; by Me if any man enter in, he shall be saved, and shall go in and out, and find pasture. The thief cometh not but for to steal and to kill and to destroy; I am come that they might have life, and that they might have it more abundantly.

I am the Good Shepherd. The Good Shepherd giveth His life for the sheep; but he that is an hireling and not the shepherd, whose own the sheep are not, seeth the wolf coming and leaveth the sheep and fleeth; and the wolf catcheth them and scattereth the sheep. The hireling fleeth, because he is an hireling and careth not for the sheep. I am the Good Shepherd, and know My sheep, and am known of Mine. As the Father knoweth Me, even so know I the Father; and I lay down My life for the sheep. And other sheep I have, which are not of this fold; them also I must bring, and they shall hear My voice, and there shall be one fold and one Shepherd. Therefore doth My Father love Me, because I lay down My life, that I might take it again. No man taketh it from Me, but I lay it down of Myself. I have power to lay it down, and I have power to take it again. This commandment have I received of My Father.

My sheep hear my voice, and I know them, and they follow Me; and I give unto them eternal life; and they shall never perish, neither shall any man pluck them out of My hand. My Father, which gave them Me, is greater than all; and no man is able to pluck them out of My Father's hand.

# The Evening Prayer

DIVINE SAVIOR, Shepherd of our souls, embrace us with Thy love, and protect us with Thine almighty arm during the coming night as sheep of Thy fold. We need Thee, for we are wounded and bruised by sin, vexed and perplexed by the heavy tasks and burdens of the day. In Thy mercy forgive us, and heal our sin-distressed heart, and in Thy goodness uphold us amid the anxieties and cares of life.

Take us by the hand and lead us. Give us also the blessed assurance that no one shall be able to pluck us out of Thy Father's hand. Remove every doubt from our hearts, and also all unbelief. Fulfill Thy promises upon this family, children of Thy love.

Forgive us all our sins. Keep us in Thy grace. Grant us strength to abide faithful to Thee and Thy Gospel, always following Thee and serving Thee, who hast laid down Thy life to make us Thine forever. Gracious Shepherd, keep us in Thy protection until we shall stand in Thy visible presence in the glories of eternal life. Amen.

## THE EVENING HYMN

The Lord my Shepherd is,
    I shall be well supplied.
Since He is mine and I am His,
    What can I want beside?

He leads me to the place
    Where heavenly pasture grows,
Where living waters gently pass
    And full salvation flows.

If e'er I go astray,
    He doth my soul reclaim
And guides me in His own right way
    For His most holy name.

While He affords His aid,
    I cannot yield to fear;
Though I should walk through
        death's dark shade,
    My Shepherd's with me there.

Amid surrounding foes
  Thou dost my table spread;
My cup with blessing overflows,
  And joy exalts my head.

The bounties of Thy love
  Shall crown my following days,
Nor from Thy house will I remove
  Nor cease to speak Thy praise.
                          Amen.

# Treasures of Hope

## THE FOURTH WEEK

# THE FOURTH WEEK

## Sunday Morning

## Psalm 116

I LOVE the Lord, because He hath heard my voice and my supplications. Because He hath inclined His ear unto me, therefore will I call upon Him as long as I live. The sorrows of death compassed me, and the pains of hell gat hold upon me; I found trouble and sorrow. Then called I upon the name of the Lord: O Lord, I beseech Thee, deliver my soul. Gracious is the Lord, and righteous; yea, our God is merciful. The Lord preserveth the simple; I was brought low, and He helped me. Return unto thy rest, O my soul, for the Lord hath dealt bountifully with thee. For Thou hast delivered my soul from death, mine eyes from tears, and my feet from falling.

I will walk before the Lord in the land of the living. I believed, therefore have I spoken; I was greatly afflicted. I said in my haste, All men are liars. What shall I render unto the Lord for all His benefits toward me? I will take the cup of salvation and call upon the name of the Lord. I will pay my vows unto the Lord now in the presence of all His people.

Precious in the sight of the Lord is the death of His saints. O Lord, truly I am Thy servant; I am Thy servant and the son of Thine handmaid; Thou hast loosed my bonds. I will offer to Thee the sacrifice of thanksgiving and will call upon the name of the Lord. I will pay my vows unto the Lord now in the presence of all His people, in the courts of the Lord's house, in the midst of thee, O Jerusalem. Praise ye the Lord.

# The Morning Prayer

LORD JESUS, who on this first day of the week didst raise Thyself from the dead to live eternally, grant that we may rise by the power of the Holy Spirit out of the deadness of sin and live to praise and glorify Thee. May we this day confess Thee and worship Thee as our risen Savior and our ever-living Redeemer. We beseech Thee to prepare our hearts to receive Thy Word, the Gospel of reconciliation, and rejoice in our redemption, which has made us Thine own.

Grant, Shepherd of the flock, that all ministers of the Gospel know nothing this day but the story of Thy redeeming love, and hold before the eyes of their hearers only Thee, the uplifted and crucified Savior. Give us the grace to praise Thee with cleansed lips and purified hearts. May our testimony draw many to Thee, who alone canst save, and give life eternal to, sinful man. Amen.

## THE MORNING HYMN

Love Divine, all love excelling,
Joy of heaven, to earth come down.
Fix in us Thy humble dwelling,
All Thy faithful mercies crown.
Jesus! Thou art all compassion,
Pure, unbounded love Thou art;
Visit us with Thy salvation,
Enter every trembling heart.

Breathe, oh, breathe Thy loving Spirit
Into every troubled breast!
Let us all in Thee inherit,
Let us find the promised rest.
Take away the love of sinning;
Alpha and Omega be;
End of faith as its beginning,
Set our hearts at liberty.

Finish, then, Thy new creation;
Pure and spotless let us be.
Let us see Thy great salvation
Perfectly restored in Thee,
Changed from glory into glory,
Till in heaven we take our place,
Till we cast our crowns before Thee,
Lost in wonder, love, and praise.

# Sunday Evening

## Luke 15

AND He said, A certain man had two sons; and the younger of them said to his father, Father, give me the portion of goods that falleth to me. And he divided unto them his living. And not many days after, the younger son gathered all together, and took his journey into a far country, and there wasted his substance with riotous living.

And when he had spent all, there arose a mighty famine in that land; and he began to be in want. And he went and joined himself to a citizen of that country; and he sent him into his fields to feed swine. And he would fain have filled his belly with the husks that the swine did eat; and no man gave unto him.

And when he came to himself, he said, How many hired servants of my father's have bread enough and to spare, and I perish with hunger! I will arise and go to my father, and will say unto him, Father, I have sinned against Heaven and before thee, and am no more worthy to be called thy son; make me as one of thy hired servants. And he arose and came to his father.

But when he was yet a great way off, his father saw him, and had compassion, and ran, and fell on his neck, and kissed him. And the son said unto him, Father, I have sinned against Heaven and in thy sight, and am no more worthy to be called thy son. But the father said to his servants, Bring forth the best robe and put it on him; and put a ring on his hand and shoes on his feet; and bring hither the fatted calf and kill it; and let us eat and be merry; for this my son was dead and is alive again; he was lost and is found. And they began to be merry.

Now, his elder son was in the field; and as he came and drew nigh to the house, he heard music and dancing. And he called one of the servants and asked what these things meant. And he said unto him, Thy brother is come, and thy father hath killed the fatted calf because he hath received him safe and sound. And he was angry and would not go in; therefore came his father out and intreated him. And he, answering, said to his father, Lo, these many years do I serve thee, neither transgressed I at any time thy commandment; and yet thou never gavest me a kid that I might make merry with my friends; but as soon as this thy son was come, which hath devoured thy living with harlots, thou hast killed for him the fatted calf. And he said unto him, Son, thou art ever with me, and all that I have is thine. It was meet that we should make merry and be glad: for this thy brother was dead and is alive again, and was lost and is found.

# The Evening Prayer

HEAVENLY FATHER, who in Christ Jesus hast revealed Thy unbounded love, keep us in Thy saving grace and His redeeming wounds. Those who have erred and wandered away from Thy fold, enticed by the allurements of Satan and the world, bring back into Thy household of grace. Grant that at no time we be deceived by the wiles of Satan and the false promises of the world.

O Lord, protect us from unbelief and sin. Open our eyes to see the emptiness of life without Thee, and the hopelessness of our day if we had not the Gospel of peace proclaimed to us. Blot out our sins, and draw us with constraining love closer to Thyself. Through Thy Word and Sacrament Thou hast strengthened us for the coming week. Grant that we grow in the Christian graces of love, peace, soberness, contentment. Make us thoughtful and considerate, forgiving

those who have offended us. Remove from
our hearts all malice and envy. May we rejoice with Thee and the angels of heaven over
the return of all erring prodigals. Receive
them and keep them with us in Thy grace
through Jesus Christ, our Lord. Amen.

## THE EVENING HYMN

Just as I am, without one plea
But that Thy blood was shed for me
And that Thou bidd'st me come to Thee,
   O Lamb of God, I come, I come.

Just as I am and waiting not
To rid my soul of one dark blot,
To Thee, whose blood can cleanse each spot,
   O Lamb of God, I come, I come.

Just as I am, though tossed about
With many a conflict, many a doubt,
Fightings and fears within, without,
   O Lamb of God, I come, I come.

Just as I am—poor, wretched, blind—
Sight, riches, healing of the mind,
Yea, all I need, in Thee to find,
   O Lamb of God, I come, I come.

Just as I am — Thou wilt receive,
Wilt welcome, pardon, cleanse, relieve;
Because Thy promise I believe,
    O Lamb of God, I come, I come.

Just as I am — Thy love unknown
Has broken every barrier down.
Now to be Thine, yea, Thine alone,
    O Lamb of God, I come, I come. Amen.

# Monday Morning

## Psalm 37

FRET not thyself because of evildoers,
neither be thou envious against the work-
ers of iniquity. For they shall soon be cut
down like the grass, and wither as the green
herb. Trust in the Lord and do good; so shalt
thou dwell in the land, and verily thou shalt
be fed. Delight thyself also in the Lord; and
He shall give thee the desires of thine heart.
Commit thy way unto the Lord; trust also in
Him, and He shall bring it to pass. And He

shall bring forth thy righteousness as the light, and thy judgment as the noonday. Rest in the Lord and wait patiently for Him; fret not thyself because of him who prospereth in his way, because of the man who bringeth wicked devices to pass. Cease from anger and forsake wrath; fret not thyself in any wise to do evil. For evildoers shall be cut off; but those that wait upon the Lord, they shall inherit the earth.

For yet a little while, and the wicked shall not be; yea, thou shalt diligently consider his place, and it shall not be. But the meek shall inherit the earth and shall delight themselves in the abundance of peace. The wicked plotteth against the just, and gnasheth upon him with his teeth. The Lord shall laugh at him; for he seeth that his day is coming.

A little that a righteous man hath is better than the riches of many wicked. For the arms of the wicked shall be broken, but the

Lord upholdeth the righteous. The Lord knoweth the days of the upright, and their inheritance shall be forever. They shall not be ashamed in the evil time, and in the days of famine they shall be satisfied. But the wicked shall perish, and the enemies of the Lord shall be as the fat of lambs; they shall consume, into smoke shall they consume away. The wicked borroweth, and payeth not again, but the righteous showeth mercy and giveth. For such as be blessed of Him shall inherit the earth, and they that be cursed of Him shall be cut off. The steps of a good man are ordered by the Lord; and He delighteth in his way. Though he fall, he shall not be utterly cast down; for the Lord upholdeth him with His hand. I have been young and now am old; yet have I not seen the righteous forsaken, nor his seed begging bread. He is ever merciful and lendeth, and his seed is blessed. The Law of his God is in his heart; none of his steps shall slide.

# The Morning Prayer

OUT of the depth, O Lord, cry we to Thee, asking for help and pleading for mercy. Thou alone art our sure Refuge and everlasting Strength amid the fretful anxieties and disturbing cares of life. In Thee do we put our trust. Thou hast promised to be with us as we pass through the troubled waters of the day and week. Let us see the graciousness of Thy hand and find relaxation and shelter under Thy wings of mercy.

Graciously forgive us our trespasses, and keep us from falling into sin this day. Be with all Thy children as they face the hard things of life, and let them find encouragement and peace in Thy promises.

Bless this household, and remove from our hearts all resentful and fretful and envious thoughts. Give us a forgiving spirit and make us thoughtful, kindhearted, and gracious, even as was our Lord and Savior when He walked among men. Amen.

## THE MORNING HYMN

What God ordains is always good;
　His will abideth holy.
As He directs my life for me,
　I follow meek and lowly.
My God indeed
In every need
Doth well know how to shield me;
To Him, then, I will yield me.

What God ordains is always good.
　His loving thought attends me;
No poison can be in the cup
　That my Physician sends me.
My God is true;
Each morn anew
I'll trust His grace unending,
My life to Him commending.

What God ordains is always good.
　He is my Friend and Father;
He suffers naught to do me harm,
　Though many storms may gather.
Now I may know
Both joy and woe,
Some day I shall see clearly
That He hath loved me dearly. Amen.

# Monday Evening

## Psalm 40

I WAITED patiently for the Lord, and He inclined unto me and heard my cry. He brought me up also out of a horrible pit, out of the miry clay, and set my feet upon a rock and established my goings. And He hath put a new song in my mouth, even praise unto our God; many shall see it, and fear and shall trust in the Lord. Blessed is that man that maketh the Lord his Trust and respecteth not the proud nor such as turn aside to lies. Many, O Lord my God, are Thy wonderful works which Thou hast done and Thy thoughts which are to usward; they cannot be reckoned up in order unto Thee. If I would declare and speak of them, they are more than can be numbered. Sacrifice and offering Thou didst not desire; mine ears hast Thou opened; burnt offering and sin offering hast Thou not required.

Then said I, Lo, I come; in the Volume of the Book it is written of Me. I delight to do Thy will, O My God; yea, Thy Law is within my heart. I have preached righteousness in the great congregation; lo, I have not refrained My lips, O Lord, Thou knowest. I have not hid Thy righteousness within My heart; I have declared Thy faithfulness and Thy salvation; I have not concealed Thy loving-kindness and Thy truth from the great congregation.

Withhold not Thou Thy tender mercies from Me, O Lord; let Thy loving-kindness and Thy truth continually preserve Me. For innumerable evils have compassed Me about; Mine iniquities have taken hold upon Me, so that I am not able to look up; they are more than the hairs of Mine head; therefore My heart faileth Me. Be pleased, O Lord, to deliver Me; O Lord, make haste to help Me. Let them be ashamed and confounded together that seek after My soul to destroy it; let them be driven backward and put to shame that wish Me evil. Let them be desolate for a reward of their shame that say unto Me, Aha, aha! Let all those that seek Thee rejoice and be glad in Thee; let such as love Thy salvation say continually, The Lord be magnified. But I am poor and needy; yet the Lord thinketh upon Me: Thou art My Help and My Deliverer; make no tarrying, O My God.

# The Evening Prayer

MOST GRACIOUS LORD, who dost uphold all things with Thine almighty arm and who promisest protection under Thy gracious wings, think upon us and let us rest safely in Thy divine benediction. Watch over us, Thou who dost neither slumber nor sleep. Help us to accept Thy judgments, which are wiser and higher than our own. Remove all vexations and irritations from our household.

Have mercy upon us, and let Thy face shine upon us in this evening hour.

We are mindful of our many shortcomings, and we know that we cannot hide them from Thee. But Thou hast graciously promised to pardon abundantly; for Jesus' sake put all our sins out of Thy remembrance.

Without Thee life would be hopeless and hapless, but Thy presence brings to us joy and peace. Fulfill all Thy promises upon us as we patiently wait on Thee and rejoice in our salvation, which has been made certain and sure by Christ's death on the Cross and His glorious resurrection from the dead. Amen, we wait on Thee, O Lord. Amen.

## THE EVENING HYMN

I am trusting Thee, Lord Jesus,
   Trusting only Thee;
Trusting Thee for full salvation,
   Great and free.

I am trusting Thee for pardon;
   At Thy feet I bow,
For Thy grace and tender mercy
   Trusting now.

I am trusting Thee for cleansing
   In the crimson flood,
Trusting Thee to make me holy
   By Thy blood.

I am trusting Thee to guide me;
   Thou alone shalt lead,
Every day and hour supplying
   All my need. Amen.

# Tuesday Morning

## I Corinthians 15

BY the grace of God I am what I am, and
His grace which was bestowed upon me
was not in vain; but I labored more abundantly than they all; yet not I, but the grace
of God which was with me. Therefore,

whether it were I or they, so we preach, and so ye believed. Now, if Christ be preached that He rose from the dead, how say some among you that there is no resurrection of the dead? But if there be no resurrection of the dead, then is Christ not risen; and if Christ be not risen, then is our preaching vain, and your faith is also vain. Yea, and we are found false witnesses of God, because we have testified of God that He raised up Christ, whom He raised not up, if so be that the dead rise not. For if the dead rise not, then is not Christ raised; and if Christ be not raised, your faith is vain, ye are yet in your sins. Then they also which are fallen asleep in Christ are perished.

If in this life only we have hope in Christ, we are of all men most miserable. But now is Christ risen from the dead and become the Firstfruits of them that slept. For since by man came death, by man came also the resurrection of the dead. For as in Adam all die,

even so in Christ shall all be made alive.
But every man in his own order: Christ the
Firstfruits; afterward they that are Christ's
at His coming. Then cometh the end, when
He shall have delivered up the Kingdom to
God, even the Father, when He shall have
put down all rule and all authority and
power. For He must reign, till He hath put
all enemies under His feet. The last enemy
that shall be destroyed is death.

# The Morning Prayer

LORD JESUS, risen and ever-living Savior, with Thee and by Thy grace we have
risen to a newness of life and have been made
heirs of Thine eternal glory. In adoration we
come to Thee, acknowledging Thee as our
Lord and God, our living and ascended Savior, and King of heaven and earth and eternity.

We praise Thee, who hast conquered sin
and death by crushing the serpent's head. We

thank Thee for the glorious hope of life ever-lasting. With the saints of all ages we, too, confess: "I believe in the resurrection of the body and the life everlasting." This we know to be true because Thou didst come forth on the third day from the tomb and didst show Thyself alive to many both in Jerusalem and in Galilee.

We beseech Thee to strengthen our faith that we may with joy look forward to our redemption from the sorrows and tears of life. Grant that we remember at all times that we are pilgrims and strangers in this present world but have an abiding place in Thy presence where all disappointments and heartaches and crying shall cease. O Lord, who art the Resurrection and the Life, abide with us in life and death and bring us at last into Thy presence, that with all the saints and angels we may praise and worship Thee in endless glory forevermore. Amen.

## THE MORNING HYMN

"Christ the Lord is risen today,"
Sons of men and angels say.
Raise your joys and triumphs high;
Sing, ye heavens, and, earth, reply.

Love's redeeming work is done,
Fought the fight, the battle won.
Lo, our Sun's eclipse is o'er;
Lo, He sets in blood no more.

Vain the stone, the watch, the seal;
Christ has burst the gates of hell.
Death in vain forbids His rise;
Christ has opened Paradise.

Lives again our glorious King;
Where, O Death, is now thy sting?
Once He died our souls to save;
Where thy victory, O Grave?

Hail the Lord of earth and heaven!
Praise to Thee by both be given!
Thee we greet triumphant now:
Hail, the Resurrection Thou! Amen.

# Tuesday Evening

## Psalm 146

PRAISE ye the Lord. Praise the Lord, O my soul. While I live, will I praise the Lord; I will sing praises unto my God while I have any being. Put not your trust in princes nor in the son of man, in whom there is no help His breath goeth forth, he returneth to his earth; in that very day his thoughts perish.

Happy is he that hath the God of Jacob for his help, whose hope is in the Lord, his God, which made heaven and earth, the sea and all that therein is; which keepeth truth forever; which executeth judgment for the oppressed; which giveth food to the hungry. The Lord looseth the prisoners; the Lord openeth the eyes of the blind; the Lord raiseth them that are bowed down; the Lord loveth the righteous; the Lord preserveth the strangers; He relieveth the fatherless and widow; but the way of the wicked He turneth upside down.

The Lord shall reign forever, even thy God, O Zion, unto all generations. Praise ye the Lord!

# The Evening Prayer

WITH all our heart we praise Thee, Creator of all things visible and invisible, who art also our Father in Christ Jesus, loving us and forgiving us all sins of the day. To know that Thou art thinking of us and art holding us in the hollow of Thy hand enables us to find rest and sleep without fear and misgivings. Shine Thou into our hearts with Thy forgiving love and rule therein with Thine eternal peace in Christ Jesus.

Watch over the fatherless and widows. Protect those who travel by land, sea, and air. Be present at the bedside of all the suffering and sick. Let Thy holy angels take to glory those who are dying in faith.

Accept our thanks and praise which we offer to Thee at the close of the day — and take every unforgiving and malicious thought from us. Give peace to all mankind and let Thy saving truth reach the ends of the earth, that all the generations of men may praise Thee from continent to continent in Christ Jesus, the Savior of all. Amen.

## THE EVENING HYMN

Praise to the Lord, the Almighty, the
    King of Creation!
O my soul, praise Him, for He is thy
    Health and Salvation.
Join the full throng;
Wake, harp and psalter and song;
    Sound forth in glad adoration.

Praise to the Lord, who o'er all things
    so wondrously reigneth,

Who, as on wings of an eagle, uplifteth,
    sustaineth.

Hast thou not seen

How thy desires all have been
    Granted in what He ordaineth?

Praise to the Lord, who doth prosper
    thy work and defend thee;

Who from the heavens the streams of
    His mercy doth send thee.

Ponder anew

What the Almighty can do,
    Who with His love doth befriend thee.

Praise to the Lord! Oh, let all that is
    in me adore Him!

All that hath life and breath, come
    now with praises before Him!

Let the Amen

Sound from His people again;
    Gladly for aye we adore Him. Amen.

# 𝔚ednesday 𝔐orning
## Psalm 55

GIVE ear to my prayer, O God, and hide not Thyself from my supplication. Attend unto me and hear me; I mourn in my complaint and make a noise because of the voice of the enemy, because of the oppression of the wicked; for they cast iniquity upon me, and in wrath they hate me. My heart is sore pained within me, and the terrors of death are fallen upon me. Fearfulness and trembling are come upon me, and horror hath overwhelmed me. And I said, Oh, that I had wings like a dove! for then would I fly away and be at rest. Lo, then would I wander far off and remain in the wilderness. Selah.

I would hasten my escape from the windy storm and tempest. Destroy, O Lord, and divide their tongues, for I have seen violence and strife in the city. Day and night they go about it upon the walls thereof; mischief also and sorrow are in the midst of it. Wickedness is in the midst thereof; deceit and guile depart not from her streets.

For it was not an enemy that reproached me; then I could have borne it. Neither was it he that hated me that did magnify himself against me; then I would have hid myself from him. But it was thou, a man mine equal, my guide, and mine acquaintance. We took sweet counsel together and walked unto the house of God in company. Let death seize upon them, and let them go down quick into hell; for wickedness is in their dwellings and among them. As for me, I will call upon God; and the Lord shall save me.

Evening and morning and at noon will I pray and cry aloud; and He shall hear my voice. Cast thy burden upon the Lord, and He shall sustain thee; He shall never suffer the righteous to be moved.

# The Morning Prayer

IN this morning hour we pause to receive Thy benediction, Lord, who art God from everlasting to all eternity. In Thee is rest and peace and safety. From hour to hour Thou dost stretch forth Thine hand to guide and protect us from the wiles of Satan and the allurements of a sinning world.

Bless us as we perform our day-by-day duties. Amid the vexing and irritating problems let us not become peevish and sullen. Fill our hearts and minds with cheerful thoughts. Make us more trustful of Thy mercies and promises of help. Remove all envy, bickering, and malice from our lives and let the day be rich in service to Thee and our fellow men.

Grant that each one of our household may return safely in the evening hour, unharmed in body and unshaken in faith. Hear our prayers, which we make in Jesus' name. Amen.

## THE MORNING HYMN

What a Friend we have in Jesus,
  All our sins and griefs to bear!
What a privilege to carry
  Everything to God in prayer!
Oh, what peace we often forfeit,
  Oh, what needless pain we bear,
All because we do not carry
  Everything to God in prayer!

Have we trials and temptations?
  Is there trouble anywhere?
We should never be discouraged,
  Take it to the Lord in prayer.
Can we find a friend so faithful,
  Who will all our sorrows share?
Jesus knows our every weakness—
  Take it to the Lord in prayer.

Are we weak and heavy laden,
  Cumbered with a load of care?
Precious Savior, still our Refuge—
  Take it to the Lord in prayer.
Do thy friends despise, forsake thee?
  Take it to the Lord in prayer;
In His arms He'll take and shield thee,
  Thou wilt find a solace there.
                              Amen.

# Wednesday Evening

## Psalm 96

O SING unto the Lord a new song; sing unto the Lord, all the earth. Sing unto the Lord, bless His name; show forth His salvation from day to day. Declare His glory among the heathen, His wonders among all people. For the Lord is great and greatly to be praised; He is to be feared above all gods. For all the gods of the nations are idols, but the Lord made the heavens. Honor and majesty are before Him; strength and beauty are in His sanctuary.

Give unto the Lord, O ye kindreds of the people, give unto the Lord glory and strength. Give unto the Lord the glory due unto His name; bring an offering and come into His courts. Oh, worship the Lord in the beauty of holiness; fear before Him, all the earth. Say among the heathen that the Lord reign-

eth; the world also shall be established that
it shall not be moved; He shall judge the
people righteously.

Let the heavens rejoice, and let the earth
be glad; let the sea roar, and the fullness
thereof. Let the field be joyful, and all that is
therein; then shall all the trees of the wood
rejoice before the Lord; for He cometh, for
He cometh to judge the earth; He shall judge
the world with righteousness, and the people
with His truth.

# The Evening Prayer

JESUS, most compassionate Savior, at the
close of the day we praise Thee with grateful hearts, mindful of Thy many mercies
which we have enjoyed throughout the day.
Our lives are filled with joy because Thou
hast redeemed us through Thy Cross on
Calvary. Peace comes to our souls because
Thou dost abundantly pardon. Grant that no

sins remain unforgiven as we seek sleep and rest for the night.

With Thy love draw us closer to Thee and keep us safe in Thy fold, steadfast in faith. Let us not be shaken by doubts, irritated by disappointments, and harassed by worries and anxious thoughts. Put upon our lips and in our hearts the hymn of forgiveness, that we may praise Thee with joyful songs. Savior of all mankind, speak forgiveness and peace to every weary and troubled soul; then joy shall fill homes and heaven now and forevermore. Amen.

## THE EVENING HYMN

Oh, worship the King all glorious above;
Oh, gratefully sing His power and His love,
Our Shield and Defender, the Ancient of
    of Days,
Pavilioned in splendor and girded with
    praise.

Oh, tell of His might, oh, sing of His grace,
Whose robe is the light, whose canopy
    space!
His chariots of wrath the deep thunderclouds
    form,
And dark is His path on wings of the storm.

Thy bountiful care what tongues can recite?
It breathes in the air, it shines in the light,
It streams from the hills, it descends to the
    plain,
And sweetly distills in the dew and the rain.

Frail children of dust and feeble as frail,
In Thee do we trust nor find Thee to fail.
Thy mercies, how tender, how firm to the end,
Our Maker, Defender, Redeemer, and Friend!

O measureless Might, ineffable Love,
While angels delight to hymn Thee above,
Thy humbler creation, though feeble their
    lays,
With true adoration shall sing to Thy praise.
                           Amen.

# Thursday Morning

## I Timothy 6

GODLINESS with contentment is great gain; for we brought nothing into this world, and it is certain we can carry nothing out. And having food and raiment, let us be therewith content. But they that will be rich fall into temptation and a snare and into many foolish and hurtful lusts, which drown men in destruction and perdition. For the love of money is the root of all evil; which while some coveted after, they have erred from the faith and pierced themselves through with many sorrows.

But thou, O man of God, flee these things and follow after righteousness, godliness, faith, love, patience, meekness. Fight the good fight of faith; lay hold on eternal life, whereunto thou art also called, and hast professed a good profession before many witnesses. I give thee charge in the sight of God, who quickeneth all things, and before Christ Jesus, who before Pontius Pilate witnessed a good confession, that thou keep this commandment without spot, unrebukeable, until the appearing of our Lord Jesus Christ, which in His times He shall show, who is the blessed and only Potentate, the King of Kings and Lord of Lords; who only hath immortality, dwelling in the light which no man can approach unto; whom no man hath seen nor can see; to whom be honor and power everlasting. Amen.

# The Morning Prayer

E TERNAL Caretaker of body and soul, we acknowledge with thankful hearts that we are Thine alone by grace. We have brought nothing with us into the world but a sinful nature and a rebellious heart. By the baptismal grace of the Holy Spirit we have been reborn and enriched with many spiritual blessings, which Thy Son purchased for us on the accursed tree of Golgotha.

Grant us this day the fullness of Thy forgiveness, the blessedness of Thy peace, the comfort of Thy promises, and the joy of Thy salvation.

We confess that we are not deserving of these treasures of grace. We have been indifferent and careless times without number. The allurements of the world have enticed us, and we have been too busy gathering in our daily bread. Today give us grace to withstand the temptations of this world and the lust for gold and honor. May we serve Thee with all our heart through Jesus Christ, our Lord. Amen.

## THE MORNING HYMN

Thee will I love, my Strength, my Tower;
 Thee will I love, my Hope, my Joy;
Thee will I love with all my power,
 With ardor time shall ne'er destroy.
Thee will I love, O Light Divine,
So long as life is mine.

Thee will I love, my Life, my Savior,
 Who art my best and truest Friend;
Thee will I love and praise forever,
 For never shall Thy kindness end;
Thee will I love with all my heart,
Thou my Redeemer art.

Oh, teach me, Lord, to love Thee truly
 With soul and body, head and heart,
And grant me grace that I may duly
 Practice fore'er love's sacred art.
Grant that my every thought may be
Directed e'er to Thee.

Thee will I love, my Crown of gladness,
 Thee will I love, my God and Lord,
Amid the darkest depths of sadness;
 Nor for the hope of high reward—
For Thine own sake, O Light Divine,
So long as life is mine. Amen.

# Thursday Evening

## Psalm 50

THE mighty God, even the Lord, hath spoken and called the earth from the rising of the sun unto the going down thereof. Out of Zion, the perfection of beauty, God hath shined. Our God shall come and shall not keep silence; a fire shall devour before Him, and it shall be very tempestuous round about him. He shall call to the heavens from above and to the earth, that He may judge His people.

Gather My saints together unto Me, those that have made a covenant with Me by sacrifice. And the heavens shall declare His righteousness, for God is Judge Himself. Selah.

Hear, O My people, and I will speak; O Israel, and I will testify against thee; I am God, even thy God. I will not reprove thee for thy sacrifices or thy burnt offerings to have been continually before Me. I will take no bullock out of thy house nor he-goats out of thy folds. For every beast of the forest is Mine, and the cattle upon a thousand hills. I know all the fowls of the mountains, and the wild beasts of the field are Mine. If I were hungry, I would not tell thee; for the world is Mine, and the fullness thereof. Will I eat the flesh of bulls or drink the blood of goats? Offer unto God thanksgiving, and pay thy vows unto the Most High, and call upon Me in the day of trouble; I will deliver thee, and thou shalt glorify Me.

But unto the wicked God saith, What hast thou to do to declare My statutes, or that thou shouldest take My covenant in thy mouth, seeing thou hatest instruction, and castest My words behind thee? When thou sawest a thief, then thou consentedst with him, and hast been partaker with adulterers:

Thou givest thy mouth to evil, and thy tongue frameth deceit. Thou sittest and speakest against thy brother; thou slanderest thine own mother's son. These things hast thou done, and I kept silence; thou thoughtest that I was altogether such an one as thyself. But I will reprove thee and set them in order before thine eyes. Now consider this, ye that forget God, lest I tear you in pieces and there be none to deliver. Whoso offereth praise glorifieth Me; and to him that ordereth his conversation aright will I shew the salvation of God.

# The Evening Prayer

LORD GOD, we, Thy children of grace and heirs of the redemption in Christ Jesus, give thanks and praise to Thee because Thou hast been with us through the years, providing us with daily bread and sustaining our faith through Thy Word of salvation. Thy goodness has preserved us in the day of trouble, and Thy mercy has forgiven us our daily trespasses.

We admit and confess that our loyalty and devotion to Thee has not been what it ought to be. We have been neglectful in prayer, unmindful of Thy grace, slow in service and sacrifice. Forgive us, O Lord. Keep us ever united with Thy holy Christian Church until we enter the Church Triumphant of eternity.

Shield us with Thy protecting arm this coming night, that we may be refreshed by a restful sleep and awake stronger in body, more alert in mind, and make us confident at all times of Thy love in Christ Jesus, our Shepherd and Friend. Amen.

## THE EVENING HYMN

Now thank we all our God
  With heart and hands and voices,
Who wondrous things hath done,
  In whom His world rejoices;
Who from our mother's arms
  Hath blessed us on our way
With countless gifts of love
  And still is ours today.

Oh, may this bounteous God
  Through all this life be near us
With ever joyful hearts
  And blessed peace to cheer us,
And keep us in His grace,
  And guide us when perplexed,
And free us from all ills
  In this world and the next.

All praise and thanks to God
  The Father now be given,
The Son, and Him who reigns
  With them in highest heaven:
The one eternal God,
  Whom earth and heaven adore!
For thus it was, is now,
  And shall be evermore. Amen.

# Friday Morning

## Hebrews 11

BY FAITH Moses, when he was come to years, refused to be called the son of Pharaoh's daughter, choosing rather to suffer affliction with the people of God than to enjoy the pleasures of sin for a season, esteeming the reproach of Christ greater riches than the treasures in Egypt; for he had respect unto the recompense of the reward. By faith he forsook Egypt, not fearing the wrath of the king; for he endured as seeing Him who is invisible. Through faith he kept the Passover and the sprinkling of blood, lest He that destroyed the firstborn should touch them. By faith they passed through the Red Sea as by dry land, which the Egyptians assaying to do were drowned.

By faith the walls of Jericho fell down after they were compassed about seven days.

By faith the harlot Rahab perished not with them that believed not, when she had received the spies with peace. And what shall I more say? For the time would fail me to tell of Gedeon, and of Barak, and of Samson, and of Jephthae; of David also, and Samuel, and of the Prophets; who through faith subdued kingdoms, wrought righteousness, obtained promises, stopped the mouths of lions, quenched the violence of fire, escaped the edge of the sword, out of weakness were made strong, waxed valiant in fight, turned to flight the armies of the aliens. Women received their dead raised to life again; and others were tortured, not accepting deliverance, that they might obtain a better resurrection; and others had trial of cruel mockings and scourgings, yea, moreover of bonds and imprisonment. They were stoned; they were sawn asunder, were tempted, were slain with the sword; they wandered about in sheepskins and goatskins, being destitute, afflicted, tormented (of whom the world was not worthy); they wandered in deserts and in mountains and in dens and caves of the earth. And these all, having obtained a good report through faith, received not the promise, God having provided some better thing for us, that they without us should not be made perfect.

# The Morning Prayer

LORD, who through the ages hast protected Thy saints, direct our lives today that we may not err from the narrow way which leads to life eternal. Grant that we may choose at all times to do Thy will, suffering rather the disfavor of the world than offending against Thy gracious love. Make us more than conquerors as we face opposition, ridicule, and persecution of those who hate Thy name and despise Thy Son, Jesus Christ, our Savior. Give us the necessary courage and boldness to confess Him who died for our redemption on Calvary.

Forgive us wherever we have been ashamed of Thee and denied Jesus as our Redeemer and Lord. Help us to bear witness by word and action of the hope that is within us, that Jesus, Thy Son, may confess us before Thy throne in the glories of heaven. Amen.

## THE MORNING HYMN

The Son of God goes forth to war
  A kingly crown to gain.
His blood-red banner streams afar;
  Who follows in His train?
Who best can drink His cup of woe,
  Triumphant over pain,
Who patient bears his cross below,
  He follows in His train.

The martyr* first, whose eagle eye
  Could pierce beyond the grave,
Who saw his Master in the sky
  And called on Him to save.
Like Him, with pardon on His tongue,
  In midst of mortal pain,
He prayed for them that did the wrong—
  Who follows in his train?

A glorious band, the chosen few,
  On whom the Spirit came,
Twelve valiant saints; their hope they knew
  And mocked the cross and flame.
They met the tyrant's brandished steel,
  The lion's gory mane;
They bowed their necks the death to feel—
  Who follows in their train?

A noble army, men and boys,
  The matron and the maid,
Around the Savior's throne rejoice,
  In robes of light arrayed.
They climbed the steep ascent of heaven
  Through peril, toil, and pain.
O God, to us may grace be given
  To follow in their train. Amen.

*Stephen

# 𝔉riday 𝔈vening

## Psalm 71

IN Thee, O Lord, do I put my trust; let me
never be put to confusion. Deliver me in
Thy righteousness and cause me to escape;
incline Thine ear unto me and save me. Be
Thou my strong Habitation, whereunto I
may continually resort; Thou hast given
commandment to save me; for Thou art my
Rock and my Fortress. Deliver me, O my
God, out of the hand of the wicked, out of
the hand of the unrighteous and cruel man.
For Thou art my Hope, O Lord God; Thou
art my Trust from my youth. By Thee have
I been holden up from the womb; Thou art
He that took me out of my mother's bowels;
my praise shall be continually of Thee. I am
as a wonder unto many, but Thou art my
strong Refuge. Let my mouth be filled with
Thy praise and with Thy honor all the day.

Cast me not off in the time of old age; forsake me not when my strength faileth. For mine enemies speak against me, and they that lay wait for my soul take counsel together, saying, God hath forsaken him; persecute and take him, for there is none to deliver him. O God, be not far from me; O my God, make haste for my help. Let them be confounded and consumed that are adversaries to my soul; let them be covered with reproach and dishonor that seek my hurt. But I will hope continually and will yet praise Thee more and more. My mouth shall show forth Thy righteousness and Thy salvation all the day, for I know not the numbers thereof. I will go in the strength of the Lord God; I will make mention of Thy righteousness, even of Thine only.

O God, Thou has taught me from my youth, and hitherto have I declared Thy wondrous works. Now also, when I am old and gray-headed, O God, forsake me not, until I

have showed Thy strength unto this generation and Thy power to every one that is to
come. Thy righteousness also, O God, is very
high, who hast done great things. O God,
who is like unto Thee!

# The Evening Prayer

O MOST HOLY LORD, with each day
we draw closer to our journey's end
and nearer to the hour when we shall behold
Thee in all the glory of eternity. Fill our
hearts with the joy of that longed-for day.
Amid the trials and perplexities of life let the
hope of heaven make us patient in tribulations.

Cast us not off in our old age, but give
us the necessary strength to continue till Thy
gracious will calls us to Thyself in glory.
Provide us daily with bread and keep us in
Thy grace. We praise Thee for all the mercies shown to us from day to day.

At the close of this day let Thy benediction make our joy greater and our peace more certain. Forgive us all sin, and bless us with a restful sleep.

Grant to all Thy children protection and forgiveness. Then we shall daily praise Thee and thank Thee through Jesus Christ, the ascended and living Savior and King. Amen.

## THE EVENING HYMN

O God of Jacob, by whose hand
    Thy people still are fed,
Who through this weary pilgrimage
    Hast all our fathers led,

Our vows, our prayers, we now present
    Before Thy throne of grace;
God of our fathers, be the God
    Of their succeeding race.

Through each perplexing path of life
    Our wandering footsteps guide;
Give us each day our daily bread,
    And raiment fit provide.

Oh, spread Thy covering wings around
Till all our wanderings cease
And at our Father's loved abode
Our souls arrive in peace.

Now with the humble voice of prayer
Thy mercy we implore;
Then with a grateful voice of praise
Thy goodness we'll adore. Amen.

# Saturday Morning

## Psalm 34

I WILL bless the Lord at all times; His praise shall continually be in my mouth. My soul shall make her boast in the Lord; the humble shall hear thereof and be glad. Oh, magnify the Lord with me, and let us exalt His name together. I sought the Lord, and He heard me and delivered me from all my fears.

They looked unto Him and were lightened, and their faces were not ashamed. This poor man cried, and the Lord heard him and saved him out of all his troubles. The angel of the Lord encampeth round about them that fear Him and delivereth them. Oh, taste and see that the Lord is good; blessed is the man that trusteth in Him. Oh, fear the Lord, ye His saints, for there is no want to them that fear Him. The young lions do lack and suffer hunger; but they that seek the Lord shall not want any good thing.

Come, ye children, hearken unto me; I will teach you the fear of the Lord. What man is he that desireth life and loveth many days, that he may see good? Keep thy tongue from evil and thy lips from speaking guile. Depart from evil and do good; seek peace and pursue it. The eyes of the Lord are upon the righteous, and His ears are open unto their cry. The face of the Lord is against them that do evil, to cut off the remembrance of them from the earth. The righteous cry, and the Lord heareth and delivereth them out of all their troubles.

The Lord is nigh unto them that are of a broken heart, and saveth such as be of a contrite spirit. Many are the afflictions of the righteous, but the Lord delivereth him out of them all. He keepeth all his bones; not one of them is broken. Evil shall slay the wicked, and they that hate the righteous shall be desolate. The Lord redeemeth the soul of His servants, and none of them that trust in Him shall be desolate.

# The Morning Prayer

SAVIOR of the lost, who dost bid all the weary and heavy-laden to come to Thee, we bring all our burdens of life and our many sins to Thy feet, pleading for salvation through forgiveness, and strength through Thy guiding hand. Without Thee life is meaningless and empty; without Thee we have no refuge, no rock to which to cling, no hope.

We confess that we have not at all times appreciated Thy love nor followed and obeyed Thee with all our heart. Forgive us, gracious Friend of sinners. Preserve us in faith; make us patient in perplexing moments; guard us against all malice and evil speaking.

Hide our sins with the garment of Thy righteousness, and in Thy grace cover the multitude of our many transgressions. Keep us humble in spirit and pure in heart and noble in conduct. Let our love to Thee be reflected in our lives, that Thy name may be glorified and Thy kingdom grow and the number of Thine elect increase till all Thy saints be gathered before Thy throne of glory to praise Thee with the hallelujahs of heaven. Amen.

## THE MORNING HYMN

Awake, my soul, and with the sun
Thy daily stage of duty run;
Shake off dull sloth and joyful rise
To pay thy morning sacrifice.

All praise to Thee, who safe hast kept
And hast refreshed me while I slept.
Grant, Lord, when I from death shall wake,
I may of endless life partake.

Lord, I my vows to Thee renew;
Disperse my sins as morning dew;
Guard my first springs of thought and will
And with Thyself my spirit fill.

Direct, control, suggest, this day,
All I design or do or say,
That all my powers, with all their might,
In Thy sole glory may unite.

Praise God, from whom all blessings flow;
Praise Him, all creatures here below;
Praise Him above, ye heavenly host:
Praise Father, Son, and Holy Ghost.

                              Amen.

# Saturday Evening

## Psalm 27

THE Lord is my Light and my Salvation; whom shall I fear? The Lord is the Strength of my life; of whom shall I be afraid? When the wicked, even mine enemies and my foes, came upon me to eat up my flesh, they stumbled and fell. Though an host should encamp against me, my heart shall not fear; though war should rise against me, in this will I be confident. One thing have I desired of the Lord, that will I seek after: that I may dwell in the house of the Lord all the days of my life, to behold the beauty of the Lord and to enquire in His Temple. For in the time of trouble He shall hide me in His pavilion; in the secret of His Tabernacle shall He hide me; He shall set me up upon a rock. And now shall mine head be lifted up above mine enemies round about me; therefore will I offer in His Tabernacle sacrifices of joy; I will sing, yea, I will sing praises unto the Lord.

Hear, O Lord, when I cry with my voice; have mercy also upon me and answer me. When Thou saidst, Seek ye My face, my heart said unto Thee, Thy face, Lord, will I seek. Hide not Thy face far from me; put not Thy servant away in anger. Thou hast been my Help; leave me not, neither forsake me, O God of my salvation. When my father and my mother forsake me, then the Lord will take me up.

Teach me Thy way, O Lord, and lead me in a plain path because of mine enemies. Deliver me not over unto the will of mine enemies; for false witnesses are risen up against me, and such as breathe out cruelty. I had fainted unless I had believed to see the goodness of the Lord in the land of the living. Wait on the Lord; be of good courage, and He shall strengthen thine heart; wait, I say, on the Lord.

# The Evening Prayer

THROUGHOUT the length of days, O Lord, Thy grace has enriched our lives, and Thine open hand has supplied all our needs. Graciously hast Thou shown us the way which leads to life eternal, and through Thy Holy Spirit Thou hast opened our understanding to believe in Jesus Christ as our Lord and Savior.

With grateful hearts we praise Thee, who hast given us the Gospel of reconciliation. With eager desire we look forward to hearing Thy Word tomorrow and the blessed assurance of forgiveness and peace. Grant that the message fall upon fertile ground and abide in our hearts and lives for this coming week and beyond.

Bless all ministers and missionaries of Thy Gospel. Grant that they proclaim with joy the good news that Christ came into the world to seek and to save sinners. Permit nothing to discourage them nor cause them to become weary of the work of their high calling. Open Thou our hearts to hear and our hands to render service. May we dedicate our lives anew to Thee and as consecrated servants be a light in the world.

Hear Thou our prayer and bless our family, our church, and our nation. Then Thine shall be the glory through endless days and the honor through all eternity. Praise be to Thee, now and forever. Amen.

## THE EVENING HYMN

Abide with me! Fast falls the eventide;
The darkness deepens; Lord, with me abide.
When other helpers fail and comforts flee,
Help of the helpless, oh, abide with me!

Swift to its close ebbs out life's little day;
Earth's joys grow dim, its glories pass
     away;
Change and decay in all around I see.
O Thou, who changest not, abide with me!

I need Thy presence every passing hour;
What but Thy grace can foil the Tempter's
     power?
Who like Thyself my guide and stay can be?
Through cloud and sunshine, oh, abide with
     me!

Hold Thou Thy cross before my closing eyes,
Shine through the gloom, and point me to
     the skies.
Heaven's morning breaks, and earth's vain
     shadows flee;
In life, in death, O Lord, abide with me!
                      Amen.

# 𝔗reasures of 𝔥ope

## ALONE WITH GOD

# Alone with God

## Morning Prayer Before Communion

IN SPIRIT we are gathering with Thee, precious Savior, in the Upper Room to receive with the bread and the cup Thy sacred body and blood. Grant us grace to receive this blessed Sacrament worthily and to be strengthened in our faith that this very body was given, and this very blood shed, for the forgiveness of our sins. Cleanse us from each and every transgression, great and small, remembered and forgotten. We confess that our transgressions have been many, but Thy mercy is great above the heavens. As we come with contrite hearts, speak peace to our souls. Make us worthy and let this Sacrament be to us a blessing and a benediction. Accept us and dwell in our hearts with Thy healing peace today and to the end of days. Amen.

## THE MORNING HYMN

Come, my soul, thy suit prepare,
Jesus loves to answer prayer;
He Himself has bid thee pray,
Therefore will not say thee nay.

Thou art coming to a King,
Large petitions with thee bring;
For His grace and power are such
None can ever ask too much.

With my burden I begin:
Lord, remove this load of sin;
Let Thy blood, for sinners spilt,
Set my conscience free from guilt.

Lord, I come to Thee for rest,
Take possession of my breast;
There Thy blood-bought right maintain
And without a rival reign.

While I am a pilgrim here,
Let Thy love my spirit cheer;
As my Guide, my Guard, my Friend,
Lead me to my journey's end. Amen.

# Prayer Before Receiving the Sacrament

GRACIOUS SAVIOR, enter Thou into my heart and take full possession of me. Let no distracting thoughts, no unforgiven hurt remain within me. I come with all my sins to this blessed Sacrament to be cleansed. Accept me just as I am. Amen.

## THE MORNING HYMN

Thy Table I approach,
  Dear Savior, hear my prayer;
Oh, let no unrepented sin
  Prove hurtful to me there!

Lo, I confess my sins
  And mourn their wretched bands;
A contrite heart is sure to find
  Forgiveness at Thy hands.

Thy body and Thy blood,
  Once slain and shed for me,
Are taken here with mouth and soul
  In blest reality.

Oh, may I never fail
  To thank Thee day and night
For Thy true body and true blood,
  O God, my Peace and Light!  Amen.

# Prayer After Receiving the Sacrament

PRECIOUS Lord and Savior, with thanksgiving and praise I worship Thee, who hast come to my heart. Grant that I may rejoice in Thy presence day after day and walk continually in this newness of life. Thine I am. Keep me steadfast in faith and loyal in my service to Thee, who hast given Thy life that I might be Thine forevermore. Amen.

# THE COMMUNION HYMN

I heard the voice of Jesus say,
  "Come unto Me and rest;
Lay down, thou weary one, lay down,
  Thy head upon My breast."
I came to Jesus as I was,
  Weary and worn and sad;
I found in Him a resting place,
  And He has made me glad.

I heard the voice of Jesus say,
  "Behold, I freely give
The living water; thirsty one,
  Stoop down and drink and live."
I came to Jesus, and I drank
  Of that life-giving stream;
My thirst was quenched, my soul revived,
  And now I live in Him.

I heard the voice of Jesus say,
  "I am this dark world's Light;
Look unto Me, thy morn shall rise
  And all thy day be bright."
I looked to Jesus, and I found
  In Him my Star, my Sun;
And in that Light of Life I'll walk
  Till traveling days are done. Amen.

# Evening Prayer after Receiving Communion

JESUS, Lover of my soul, in sincere appreciation we praise Thee, who hast so graciously provided this Sacrament of Thy body and blood. In this bread and with this cup we have visible assurance of Thy forgiveness. We now abide in Thee and Thou in us. Our hearts rejoice as the burden of sin is removed and the conscience cleansed.

Grant us grace and strength to walk closer to Thee and to glorify Thy name as salt and leaven of the community. May we daily bear witness of the hope and the peace which dwell in our hearts. Preserve us in Thy grace, enrich our lives with Thy Word, and let our lips praise Thee, who hast redeemed us and in that night in which Thou wast betrayed given us this blessed Sacrament of reconciliation and peace, that throughout the ages all those crushed in spirit and

burdened with sin may come and experience
the wonders of Thy forgiving love. In Thy
name we go forward. Amen.

## THE EVENING HYMN

Thine forever, God of Love!
Hear us from Thy throne above;
Thine forever may we be
Here and in eternity!

Thine forever! O how blest
They who find in Thee their rest!
Savior, Guardian, heavenly Friend,
Oh, defend us to the end!

Thine forever, Lord of Life!
Shield us through our earthly strife;
Thou, the Life, the Truth, the Way,
Guide us to the realms of day.

Thine forever! Shepherd, keep
These Thy frail and trembling sheep
Safe alone beneath Thy care,
Let us all Thy goodness share.

Thine forever! Thou our Guide,
All our wants by Thee supplied,
All our sins by Thee forgiven;
Lead us, Lord, from earth to heaven.
                              Amen.

# PRAYERS IN TIME OF SICKNESS

## The Morning Prayer

GRACIOUS SAVIOR, in whom is forgiveness and life, healing and strength, I turn to Thee in this hour of suffering and pain, asking Thy presence and Thy help. Give me the blessed assurance that all is well because Thou art with me as my Shepherd and Friend. Remove from my heart all misgivings and fears. Give to me quiet days and restful nights. Bless me with sleep.

Grant those who wait on me cheerful hearts and ready and willing hands. Give wisdom and understanding to my physician, and let the words of comfort spoken to me by my pastor make the burden lighter and the day brighter. Take all rebellion and discontent out of my heart, and forgive me all my sins and worrisome thoughts.

Grant that all may believe that Thy healing touch can help and bless even in this hour. Bless all fellow sufferers and give them and me sufficient strength for the day. Hear Thou my cry and answer me in my distress, most gracious Savior. Amen.

## THE MORNING HYMN

Art thou weary, art thou troubled,
    Art thou sore distrest?
"Come to Me," saith One, "and, coming,
    Be at rest."

Hath He marks to lead me to Him
    If He be my Guide?
"In His feet and hands are wound-prints,
    And His side."

Hath He diadem, as Monarch,
    That His brow adorns?
"Yea, a crown, in very surety,
    But of thorns."

If I find Him, if I follow,
    What His guerdon here?
"Many a sorrow, many a labor,
    Many a tear."

If I still hold closely to Him,
  What hath He at last?
"Sorrow vanquished, labor ended,
  Jordan passed."

If I ask Him to receive me,
  Will He say me nay?
"Not till earth and not till heaven
  Pass away."

Finding, following, keeping, struggling,
  Is He sure to bless?
"Saints, apostles, prophets, martyrs,
  Answer, Yes." Amen.

# The Evening Prayer

HEAVENLY and merciful Father, Thou
hast so graciously been with me today.
Without Thy divine help I should not have
been able to take a single breath. Without the
strength coming from Thee my strength
would fail. I depend altogether on Thee, O
Lord, to heal me. Protect me in the coming
night. During the long hours of darkness be

Thou my Companion. Grant me grace to believe that Thou abidest with me every moment, and that therefore I need not face the night alone.

My thankful heart praises Thee for all the mercies shown to me in these past days, and my lips shall tell of Thy power and love that healeth the sick who trust in Thee. I appreciate every kindness shown me. Bless those who so graciously take care of me.

For the coming night I place myself into Thy hands of grace. Bless me with a refreshing sleep. Calm my nerves, and speak peace to my soul, and bring healing to my body. Remove from my mind every disturbing thought. Hear me, gracious Lord, for Jesus' sake. Amen.

## THE EVENING HYMN

O Thou from whom all goodness flows,
  I lift my heart to Thee;
In all my sorrows, conflicts, woes,
  Dear Lord, remember me.

When on my poor and burdened heart
  My sins lie heavily,
Thy pardon speak, new peace impart;
  Dear Lord, remember me.

When trials sore obstruct my way
  And ills I cannot flee,
Oh, let my strength be as my day;
  Dear Lord, remember me.

If worn with pain, disease, or grief
  This feeble body be,
Grant patience, rest, and kind relief;
  Dear Lord, remember me. Amen.

# Prayer Before an Operation

O LORD, the hour has come in which I must face this operation. In Thy name and under Thy protecting arm I can go into this darkness without fear. Thou art with me. Thou dost not slumber nor sleep while I am in this deep sleep of unconsciousness, unaware of all that is done. Guide the hand of the surgeon. Bless the nurses who take care of me.

Lord, every sin which I have committed, forgive. Bring peace to my heart, and let me build my hope on Jesus Christ and His precious blood. Then no one can separate me from Thy love.

And now, Lord God, I am at peace with Thee. Thy forgiveness is in my heart. Thou art holding me in the hollow of Thy hand and wilt not fail me. Grant that this operation be successful and helpful, and let me awaken praising Thee in Christ Jesus, my Lord. Amen.

## THE HYMN

My Jesus, as Thou wilt;
Oh, may Thy will be mine!
Into Thy hand of love
I would my all resign.
Through sorrow or through joy
Conduct me as Thine own,
And help me still to say,
My Lord, Thy will be done.

My Jesus, as Thou wilt.
Though seen through many a tear,
Let not my star of hope
Grow dim or disappear,
Since Thou on earth hast wept
And sorrowed oft alone,
If I must weep with Thee,
My Lord, Thy will be done.

My Jesus, as Thou wilt.
All shall be well for me;
Each changing future scene
I gladly trust with Thee.
Straight to my home above
I travel calmly on
And sing in life or death,
My Lord, Thy will be done.
Amen.

# Prayer After an Operation

LORD, I thank Thee that Thou hast safely seen me through this operation and hast preserved my life. Thy mercies are boundless and Thy goodness without limit. Continue to let Thy healing hand rest upon me. Grant that every thing done for me by physician and nurses will speed the day of my recovery.

Ease Thou my distress; calm my nerves; speak peace to my soul. In my suffering let me remember that my Savior endured even greater pain in the Garden to redeem and heal my soul. Keep me in Thy grace and steadfast in faith.

Thou art adding to the length of my days. Grant that I will be mindful of my duties and serve Thee in faithfulness. May Thy promises become more precious to me from day to day; and when healed, may I, by Thy grace, give more attention to Thy Word and worship Thee with greater devo-

tion and more consecrated life. Let my lips
be full of praise and my life rich in service
as I recover from this operation. Accept my
thanksgiving and praise for Jesus' sake.

Amen.

## THE HYMN

The Lord, my God, be praised,
  My Light, my Life from heaven;
My Maker, who to me
  Hath soul and body given.
My Father, who doth shield
  And keep me day by day,
Doth make each moment yield
  New blessings on my way.

The Lord, my God, be praised,
  My Trust, my Life from heaven,
The Father's own dear Son,
  Whose life for me was given;
Who for my sin atoned
  With His most precious blood;
Who giveth me by faith
  The highest heavenly good.

The Lord, my God, be praised,
My Hope, my Life from heaven,
The Spirit, whom the Son
In love to me hath given.
'Tis He revives my heart,
'Tis He that gives me power,
Help, comfort, and support
In sorrow's gloomy hour.

To Him with joyful song
Our praises we are bringing,
And with the angel throng
Thrice "Holy" we are singing.
With one united voice
The Church doth Him adore.
The Lord, my God, be praised
Now and forevermore. Amen.

# Prayer for a Convalescent

ABIDE with me, wonderful Savior and
Friend, in these days of illness, and
continue to heal me. Thou hast been good to

me in these hours of helplessness, filling my soul with peace and putting my mind at ease. Let me find comfort in Thy presence, strength in prayer, and encouragement through Thy promises. Give me the necessary patience to await the day of my recovery. Thou hast been so patient with me; teach me to be hopeful, cheerful, and trusting.

To those who wait on me and look after my comfort and welfare, grant a cheerful spirit. Give me grace to accept every kindness and thoughtful service with appreciation. Remove from me every irritation and worry, and let me look forward with joy to the day that I can again come to Thy sanctuary to worship Thee. Till then let Thy presence comfort me, and Thy Word rule my every thought, and contentment and peace fill my day. Amen, grant this, most gracious Lord. Amen.

## THE HYMN

Rejoice, my heart, be glad and sing,
 A cheerful trust maintain;
For God, the Source of everything,
 Thy Portion shall remain.

He is thy Treasure, He thy Joy,
 Thy Life and Light and Lord,
Thy Counselor when doubts annoy,
 Thy Shield and great Reward.

Why spend the day in blank despair,
 In restless thought the night?
On thy Creator cast thy care;
 He makes thy burden light.

He knows how oft a Christian weeps
 And why his tears now fall;
And in the book His mercy keeps
 These things are noted all.

His wisdom never plans in vain,
 Ne'er falters or mistakes;
All that His counsels did ordain
 A happy ending makes.

Upon thy lips, then, lay thy hand
 And trust His guiding love;
Then like a rock thy peace shall stand
 Here and in heaven above. Amen.

# A Prayer for Patience

MY FAITH looks up to Thee, compassionate Redeemer, whose goodness is new every day and whose mercies endless as eternity. I have nothing to fear, even though I am suffering and in pain, because Thou art with me. Since Thou hast gone all the way to the Cross to redeem me, I know Thou wilt not forsake me in my present distress. Teach me to wait patiently from day to day, and keep me rested and composed.

I am weak and helpless, but Thou art mighty. Look on me in grace, and touch me with Thy healing. Forgive me all my doubting thoughts, and remove from me all restlessness and discontent. Bless me with sleep. Make me confident and courageous.

In the long night watches let me find Thee, and in the daytime let me ponder on Thy goodness. O Lord, calm my shattered nerves; let Thy peace rule my heart; and

bring to my remembrance daily that Thou
hast never wearied of me nor turned from
me when I cried to Thee in my distress.
Keep me therefore close to Thee, merciful
and patient Savior. Amen.

## THE HYMN

When I survey the wondrous Cross
  On which the Prince of Glory died,
My richest gain I count but loss
  And pour contempt on all my pride.

Forbid it, Lord, that I should boast
  Save in the death of Christ, my God;
All the vain things that charm me most,
  I sacrifice them to His blood.

See, from His head, His hands, His feet,
  Sorrow and love flow mingled down.
Did e'er such love and sorrow meet
  Or thorns compose so rich a crown?

Were the whole realm of nature mine,
  That were a tribute far too small;
Love so amazing, so divine,
  Demands my soul, my life, my all.
                  Amen.

# A Prayer in Distress

LORD, Thou art always mindful of Thine own, and with tender care Thou art holding me in Thy loving and merciful hands. Out of the depth of my misery and pain I call to Thee for strength and deliverance. Hear me, O Lord, hear me!

O God, doubts and fears beset me in my distress. Satan is whispering that Thy promises are not for me because I have sinned too often against Thee. But, Lord, Thou hast said in Thy Word that all who come Thou wilt help. I come crushed, helpless, contrite. Turn not from me in my great distress, but lift me out of my suffering and ease my pain. Nothing is impossible with Thee. O Lord, help me in Thy mercy.

Forgive me all my sins; forgive me wherever I have been unmindful of Thy goodness and impatient with Thy ways. Merciful God, embrace me with Thy love, and touch me with Thy healing hand. Uphold me in this hour; put underneath Thine everlasting arms.

Glorify Thyself, eternal and merciful Father, by helping me in my distress. For Jesus' sake have mercy, and grant a peaceful rest. Amen, hear my cry, O God. Amen.

## THE HYMN

Beloved, "It is well!"
  God's ways are always right,
And perfect love is o'er them all
  Though far above our sight.

Beloved, "It is well!"
  Though deep and sore the smart,
The hand that wounds knows how to bind
  And heal the broken heart.

Beloved, "It is well!"
  Though sorrow clouds our way,
'Twill only make the joy more dear
  That ushers in the day.

Beloved, "It is well!"
  The path that Jesus trod,
Though rough and strait and dark it be,
  Leads home to heaven and God.
                  Amen.

# Comforting Promises From Scripture

COME unto Me, all ye that labor and are heavy laden, and I will give you rest. Take My yoke upon you and learn of Me, for I am meek and lowly in heart, and ye shall find rest unto your souls. For My yoke is easy, and My burden is light. Matthew 11:28-30.

Yea, I have loved thee with an everlasting love; therefore with loving-kindness have I drawn thee. Jeremiah 31:3.

I, even I, am He that blotteth out thy transgressions for Mine own sake and will not remember thy sins. Isaiah 43:25.

Lord, to whom shall we go? Thou hast words of eternal life. And we believe and are sure that Thou art that Christ, the Son of the living God. John 6:68, 69.

Therefore, being justified by faith, we have peace with God through our Lord Jesus Christ; by whom also we have access by faith into this grace wherein we stand, and rejoice in hope of the glory of God. Romans 5:1, 2.

For I am persuaded that neither death nor life, nor angels, nor principalities, nor powers, nor things present, nor things to come, nor height, nor depth, nor any other creature shall be able to separate us from the love of God which is in Christ Jesus, our Lord. Romans 8:38, 39.

These things I have spoken unto you that in Me ye might have peace. In the world ye shall have tribulation; but be of good cheer, I have overcome the world. John 16:33.

My grace is sufficient for thee, for My strength is made perfect in weakness. 2 Corinthians 12:9.

Giving thanks unto the Father, which hath made us meet to be partakers of the inheritance of the saints in light; who hath delivered us from the power of darkness, and hath translated us into the kingdom of His dear Son; in whom we have redemption through His blood, even the forgiveness of sins. Colossians 1:12-14.

Heal me, O Lord, and I shall be healed; save me, and I shall be saved; for Thou art my Praise. Jeremiah 17:14.

Come now and let us reason together, saith the Lord: though your sins be as scarlet, they shall be as white as snow; though they be red like crimson, they shall be as wool. Isaiah 1:18.

For whatsoever is born of God overcometh the world; and this is the victory that overcometh the world, even our faith. Who is he that overcometh the world but he that believeth that Jesus is the Son of God? 1 John 5:4, 5.

Fear thou not, for I am with thee; be not dismayed, for I am thy God. I will strengthen thee; yea, I will help thee; yea, I will uphold thee with the right hand of My righteousness. Isaiah 41:10.